CHURCHES...
BEFORE YOU
BUILD

William L. Couchenour

Before You Build. Copyright © 2003 by Cogun, Inc.

Table of Contents

ACKNOWLEDGMENTS

I thank Mom and Dad for their courage to follow the Lord's leading and step out into the unknown to start Cogun, Inc. Dad saw the need for a company committed to serving churches with building needs after getting involved with my grandfather's church to see them through a difficult building program in 1969. In 1995, Dad began to step away from Cogun, not to retire, but to fulfill the passion God had given him and Mom to create compassionate ministries to change the lives of the underprivileged. Their sacrifices and ever deepening relationships with God are profound examples of the power, peace and joy of lives lived in Christ.

I am deeply indebted to "The Greatest Team". At Cogun, we truly have a group of unbelievable people committed to selflessly combining their efforts and expertise to provide the greatest value of services possible in creating shelter for worship and ministry. They embody what Peter Drucker described as the purpose of an organization to "enable common men to accomplish uncommon things." It is a privilege to serve them.

I thank those who have helped to make this book a meaningful tool. Carol Henry, who assists me in my role in Cogun, has been my right hand in compiling and typing this book. And my editor, Jeff Schoch, has been invaluable in refining the thoughts and words. I appreciate our District Leadership Team, Bruce Anderson, Tim Cool, J. Alan Couchenour, Jim Couchenour and Eric Payer who always challenge me to be at my best. I thank my pastor, Rev. Doug Boquist, for his input from the perspective of a church leader. And, I thank Prodigal Media for their thoughtful insights and creativity.

I give my heartfelt appreciation to Barry Banther – a gifted consultant and valued friend. Throughout Cogun, you will find Barry's fingerprints where his ideas, admonishment and encouragement have made a positive impact on the mission of Cogun. This book is no exception.

Finally, I want to thank all the pastors and church leaders of the churches with whom I had the opportunity to personally serve. You helped me shape not only my views and perspectives on how to bring value to developing facilities for churches, but you also helped to shape my understanding of the amazing God we serve, together. I honor you – you are on the front line. If God is going to change the world, it will be through the church.

BEFORE YOU BUILD

Introduction

I credit a good friend for introducing me to the majesty of the mountains. His travels have enabled him to experience all 50 states and parts of Canada. He has seen much of the varied terrain and treasures of this country, but it is his passion for the awesome magnificence of the mountains that is contagious. I often find myself planning when I will get back to walk among their snowcapped peaks and lush valleys, to be able to breathe the purity of the air and witness stars more numerous than the sands of the beaches. Living in an area where there are no mountains, I'm forced most of the time to content myself with pictures and memories.

Over the past quarter of a century, my friend has become an accomplished climber, completing ascents in the continental United States, Canada and Alaska. In my opportunities to travel with him, he has introduced me to this sport. It is difficult to describe the exhilaration that comes from clinging to the rock, making your way pitch after pitch, with a view that stretches for miles. Experiencing a summit is intoxicating. Climbing has allowed me to experience the mountains from a more meaningful perspective.

Climbing, however, is not a sport to be taken lightly. It requires attention to every detail, both those you can control (like your equipment), and those you cannot control (like the weather). Climbing as safely as possible requires an unrelenting focus and an understanding of your resources from start to finish. Certain techniques must be understood and mastered. A successful mountain ascent demands thorough planning, preparation and common sense. But there is no substitute for an experienced guide, especially when you run into the unexpected.

A church building program is not unlike a mountain ascent. You must first select the mountain that you believe God would have you climb. Many mountains are spectacular in stature and worthy of the effort, but there is one that is best for you. You need to build a team that will carry the equipment and set the protection. Then you need to assess your resources, begin the planning and check your equipment. You need to select the experienced guides to help you find the best route. You will want to establish lines of communication so you can keep everyone informed thoroughly before and throughout your journey. Even with all this preparation, you need to be ready to react to the unanticipated challenges and modify your course as necessary.

The purpose of this book is to acquaint you with the major aspects of a building program so that you can increase the opportunity for a successful and satisfying journey. A framework of the entire process will be introduced in Chapter 2, where the various components of a building program will be discussed and analyzed. A thorough understanding of the intricacies of a building program will enable you to more proficiently navigate the appropriate route. It is important that you don't "just get through" the building program like an overweight runner struggling to finish a marathon. You want to be able to finish strong, because the purpose is not to have a new building but to provide facilities to enable the growth of the ministry.

I have attempted to use language and phrases that would have the broadest understanding across denomination lines and in varying contexts. However, synergy is one word that demands further definition so that it is not just passed off as a buzzword. A foundational element of my leadership philosophy can be found in the words of Peter Drucker, one of the foremost authors on leadership: "The purpose of an organization is to enable common men to do uncommon things." We, at Cogun, believe that we can multiply our collective efforts and abilities if we serve one another with an attitude of genuine caring and respect. The best name I have found for that multiplier is synergy.

A building program, whether it's renovation of facilities, the construction of new or a combination of both, is a significant event in the life of a congregation. A tremendous amount of time, effort, money and other resources are required for most projects. That level of expense will have a significant impact on the life of a church. If those resources are used wisely, the impact will be positive for the mission of the church. There will be exciting opportunities for bonding and growing people in the Lord as you work toward a common destination.

With God's direction and the right leadership, a building program can be a thrilling time of growth both collectively and individually. But pitfalls and crevasses of divisiveness, poor decision-making and insufficient funding can cripple a project, even fatally, if they are not avoided.

CHAPTER 1- BEFORE YOU START

You have probably heard of at least one horror story of a congregation that embarked on a building program only to find itself discouraged and disillusioned in the middle of the process. It may be a congregation that has been devastated by a split or the departure of a beloved pastor because of what took place during the building program. People are left wondering and commiserating over what happened and where they went wrong. Sometimes they are left with an insurmountable debt, or worse yet, a partially completed building and no funds to make it habitable. Unfortunately these are not urban myths. They are actual experiences of some congregations.

The reasons for the trouble vary: An unscrupulous contractor leaves a project unfinished, taking the church's money with him. An egotistical architect is interested only in building a monument for himself. A selfish member of the congregation takes advantage of power or influence to the detriment of the church. An unreasonable building department requires costly revisions to a project.

My grandfather found himself in the midst of a disastrous project in his last pastorate before retiring from a life of ministry. The building was initially designed beyond what the church could afford. The general contractor abandoned the project and the state, taking with him money that was to be used for laminated arches. My dad got involved to help complete it in a way that the congregation could afford. That event, in 1969, led to the founding of Cogun, Inc. in 1970.

The reality is that disasters caused by a lack of integrity make up only a minute percentage of failed or deficient building programs. Still, no church is immune, regardless of size or denomination. The good news is that proper management can provide a way to navigate past the potential disasters. The main reasons for a deficient building program are likely the result of three root causes: insufficient leadership, poor planning and incomplete understanding of the process. A building program's relative success rises and falls on the level of quality of these three factors.

QUALITY LEADERSHIP

Leadership is essential because a successful building program will not happen on its own. Many forces along the way will attempt to derail the project or steer it in the wrong direction. The leadership must begin with a clear understanding of the ministry goals to be accomplished in the building program so it can determine the proper course to reach them. The team must be able to see clearly where the church is and where it is headed to be able to make the common-sense decisions to keep the project on the right course. Leaders will need to be clear about their purpose and strong in their resolve to make it happen, but they will also need to be humble and be able to recognize when adjustments, even significant ones, are necessary.

The leadership will need to be given the responsibility and authority to marshal the church's resources necessary to accomplish the program. They will need to have the respect of the congregation to maintain support throughout the project. They will need to coordinate committees into a united force that will be able to clear inevitable hurdles along the way.

UNDERSTANDING THE PROCESS

It is important for the leadership to have a general understanding of the overall building process. Some churches wander into a building program with only a partial awareness of certain aspects of the process. A partial awareness forces assumptions about the remainder of the process, and these assumptions can lead to misunderstandings among church committees or with industry professionals hired to do the work. Misunderstandings can cost time and money and result in a facility that fails to meet needs or expectations.

Every approach to developing facilities carries certain advantages and variations. These approaches, sometimes called project delivery systems, become the framework for the building program. A thorough understanding of how they work and what is expected of the church is necessary in each case. An understanding of their relative risks will help the church choose the project delivery system and the industry professionals to fit the specific circumstance.

A better understanding of the process will enable you to coordinate with the industry professionals. You will know what to expect and what is expected from you, leaving nothing to fall through the cracks. You also need to understand the advantages and disadvantages of the various approaches to funding. An understanding of the process will make you aware of the activities and events that will take place so you can coordinate them in a logical, effective and time-efficient manner.

The challenges caused by insufficient leadership, an inadequate understanding of the process and poor planning rarely result in outright disasters. They more often manifest themselves in subtler ways. There are congregations that choose an inexpensive building only to find out that communicating, whether by spoken word or song, is difficult because of poor acoustics, an ill-suited sound system and noise from heating, ventilation and air conditioning. Others stretch themselves financially to erect a building but then are strapped with a mortgage they cannot afford. Some congregations build a beautiful sanctuary without realizing their biggest need was education space.

The goal of a successful building program is not just to escape disaster and avoid over-designed, under-funded and inept facilities. The goal is to maximize resources to develop the combination of facilities that best meet the ministry needs and budget parameters of the church. It's not just about steering clear of what you don't want to happen. It's about achieving the magnificent purpose to which God has called your church.

PROPER PLANNING

Proper planning is the key that good leadership uses to unlock the door that leads to the right project. There are many ways to approach the design, financing and construction of facilities. Proper planning increases the likelihood of getting the facility that best meets the ministry's needs, and it is where the real dollars are spent or saved.

The reality, in a relative sense, is that there is usually little difference in contractor prices. Costs for concrete or lumber or carpet can be thousands of dollars apart, which seems significant. But those differences become small when compared to the tens and hundreds of thousands of dollars that can be saved or spent as the result of quality planning.

A church near Tampa, Florida went to bid with four general contractors. The low bid was just under $5,000,000, and the spread of the bids was barely over 1 percent. But the budget for the project was only $2,500,000. The church subsequently hired a design/build team to develop the needed facilities in budget. The variance between contractors on the initial bid was roughly $50,000. But the difference between the two design approaches was approximately $2,500,000.

This church got on the right track for developing facilities but it cost an extra year and $500,000. **The majority of the money may be spent as the building is being erected, but the planning determines the scope of what will be spent.**

A HEALTHY START

A healthy start to a day of climbing begins with a good night's sleep and a nutritious breakfast. They don't ensure a successful climb, but they provide the strength and sustenance to thoroughly enjoy the day and to vigorously overcome unexpected difficulties along the way. Similarly, there is a healthy way to start when you are considering a building program. That healthy start begins with a look inside.

Understanding the emphasis behind an emerging building program is an important first step. Purging your motives in the early stages will help you deal objectively with each step and keep you from relying on preconceived notions that could tie you to a wrong direction. Entering into a building program out of ego, to jump-start growth or because a neighboring church just was built are unhealthy reasons to begin.

From the beginning, invite God into the proceedings so that you can purify and clarify the underlying reasons for the building program. It is important that in seeking God's will, we get ourselves to the place where we are willing to accept his direction, no matter what it may be. God, through his word, has promised to direct us and provide wisdom, as long as we are open and ready.

Sometimes a building program can be considered for good reasons, but the timing is wrong. In II Samuel 7:2, we learn that David desired to build a temple when he said to Nathan, "Here I am, living in a palace of cedar, while the ark of God remains in a tent." But later in that chapter we find that the Lord spoke to Nathan to tell David that it would be his son Solomon who would build the temple. There are times today when building seems like the right thing to do, but God says the timing is not right.

It is critical to involve God at the outset so he can purge motives and provide direction. He will help leaders keep the emphasis on the ministry of the people and not the construction of a building. He will enable you to be open to the best direction. Sometimes a congregation can meet its ministry needs through a reconfiguration of its facilities. This might not be as glamorous, but it often costs much less.

God also will give you the confidence to clear hurdles along the way. Every building program encounters difficulties, but pure motives and clear direction make it easier to pass them. A genuine openness will allow you to look at every facet of the building program. Remain open to what God has to teach you along the way.

History can provide wonderful insights about what church buildings can and should do for us. It's the logical next step. Let's look briefly at the role church facilities have played in the life of God's people in the past.

A HISTORICAL PERSPECTIVE

In the Old Testament, we find that God gave specific instructions regarding the structure for the house of God and the furnishings that would facilitate worship and sacrifice for the Israelite people. The specifications for the Ark of the Covenant to house the tablets with the Ten Commandments were specific in size and materials. The same was true for the altar, table, lamp stand and other furnishings to accompany the Ark of the Covenant.

God also was precise with his instructions for building the tabernacle, including its courtyard. The design accommodated setup and removal, which allowed for the tabernacle to move with the Israelites as they traveled the land.

More than 400 years after he delivered the Israelites out of Egypt, God gave them a time of peace under Solomon. Solomon began constructing a permanent temple that was to be completed according to very specific details: 60 cubits (about 90 feet) long, 20 cubits (about 30 feet) wide and 30 cubits (about 45 feet) high. It was to include a portico, main hall and inner sanctuary. The temple was to be built with prescribed materials, including cedar, stone and gold. Every detail was spelled out, down to the size and makeup of the ornaments. Even the manner of construction was specific: All the stones were to be dressed at the quarry so the sound of hammers would not be heard at the temple site.

For the next thousand years, this temple and subsequent synagogues served as the places where people could worship God, be instructed in his ways and have sacrifices offered for their sins.

When Jesus was crucified – at the moment of his death – the inner veil of the temple was split in two from top to bottom. This moment and Christ's subsequent resurrection changed forever how man could and would relate to God. In the process, the role of worship facilities also changed.

The veil that was split separated a place described as the holy of holies from the holy place. The veil represented a barrier that only the high priest, in accordance with ceremonial rights, could pass to access God and make sacrifices for the people. With Jesus' death as the sinless Son of God, he became our sacrifice for all time, and the temple sacrifices were no longer necessary. There was no need to have a high priest approach God on our behalf since Jesus had become our high priest, and the veil was symbolically torn in two.

The book of Acts tells us that for a few weeks after his resurrection, Christ continued to teach and have fellowship with his disciples. During that time, he gave them instructions to wait in Jerusalem for the gift of the Holy Spirit. Nearly two months after the resurrection of Christ, they were gathered in one place, just as Jesus had told them to do. The day of Pentecost came, and those in the room were filled with the Holy Spirit. God no longer dwelled in places or buildings but in the hearts of his people.

There are no further instructions in the scriptures as to the design of the buildings for worship and ministry. We see instructions for God's people to be devoted to one another and to teach and to fellowship. There are instructions to pray and to grow deep in a personal relationship with God. We are instructed to love God with every fiber of our being and to treat others as we would prefer to be treated. But there were no instructions regarding the physical facilities that were to house these functions.

It appears the early church met in homes, caves and in the open – essentially, wherever they could. The earliest buildings committed exclusively to church use were likely homes. These early church facilities were all believed to be small, domestic and secular in nature. Many people believe that this was because Christians were poor and persecuted. This most likely had an impact, but in the first 300 years, the persecution was not always intense. They may have simply chosen domestic-style facilities because they felt they best met the needs of what they felt a church should be.

Early in the 4th century, Constantine paused at the Milvian Bridge before battle. There, in a vision, he saw a cross with the inscription, "By this sign thou shalt conquer." Emperor Constantine went on to defeat his enemies, and in 313 A.D., with the Edict of Milan, he made Christianity the official religion in the Roman Empire. Some believe this was the worst thing that could happen to the church because elements of paganism and distorted rituals began to blend with the worship styles of the early church.

Early on, there were no symbols such as statues or paintings because leaders wanted to distance themselves from the idolatry of the pagans and the statues of their gods. During the growth of Christianity in the 4th century, many people came into the church from varied backgrounds, and they brought superstitions and ceremonies from the religions they had known. These intermingled with the Christians of the early church.

Many of these early 4th-century churches adopted the design of basilicas, the style of many buildings of the Roman government. Temples and other buildings began to spring up at sacred sites such as Jesus' tomb and martyrs graves. This began to spread the belief that the physical building was sacred. It seemed that the early Christians felt the religion of the Christian faith should be woven in and through their daily lives. Now it was becoming associated with a building or a place, and we began to see the split between what was deemed sacred and what was secular. The church then began to be known as the building as well as the people.

The Middle Ages perpetuated this split and further associated God with a place rather than his people. But Oct. 31, 1517, Martin

Luther began a time of Reformation. Through Calvin, the Wesleys in the 18th century, and many other missionaries, revivalists and revolutionaries, changes continued. The understandings gained through the reformation began to influence the design of facilities to accommodate these new views of the role of the building. Many of the changes in design reflected the cultural views of the day.

In the United States, we can see how beliefs shaped the design and use of buildings. We visit the houses of worship from the early days of our nation's history and see the simplicity and practicality of the structures that reflected their understanding. The Mennonites would build shelters for worship only when they outgrew the ability to meet in a home. The Puritans in New England built meeting houses that would be used for worship and other purposes. Some were specifically designed to elicit the feel of the awesome presence of God through the volume and beauty of the space. Many cathedrals exist as a testimony to skill and artistry devoted to God.

I continue to see many people who are passionate about the varying views regarding design and function of church facilities. I know some believe the structure should be simple and inexpensive. They may view it is a wise use of the Lord's money to have a building where they can have a Wednesday night dinner, a Friday night basketball tournament and a Sunday morning worship service in the same space. I know others who are equally passionate about separating the worship space from all other activities. They would never think of eating in the same space where they would meet to worship. There are yet others who believe that the building should honor God through its beauty and that worship is enhanced through the visual and aural features. Some believe that symbolism alienates potential Christ followers who don't understand the traditions and liturgy of the church; others find the liturgy and symbolism are central to worship and add richness.

WHO IS RIGHT?

I remember the sadness I felt when I found Mom and Dad were going to sell the house we had lived in from when I was in first grade. It had been the homestead for 31 years. I had many memories that were tied to that house, and I always enjoyed going back because there was a warm sense that it was home. I also have memories tied to my home church. I can take you to the very spot in that church where God dramatically changed my life. Not long ago, I visited another sanctuary, the one where I was married. It took me back to that wonderful day and caused me to reflect on the beginning that opened the door to some of my deepest joys.

There is no denying that emotion can be tied to a place. But I have realized it is much more than the place that is important. It is what happens in the place that is important. I found that I am just as at home now where Mom and Dad live as I ever was in the old homestead. I still have my memories, but the true sense of home comes from being with Mom and Dad or my brothers or sister. The church I attend now was birthed by the one where God dramatically changed my life, but no one who knows me can deny the change that took place, even though I am rarely in that original sanctuary. I don't live in the same state where I was married, but I can tell you the blessings that have taken place since then have nothing to do with a center aisle, flowers, a tuxedo or a beautiful dress. All of it has everything to do with God's dwelling in us and his concern and impact on every part of our lives.

A prominent picture of an old country church hangs in the lobby of our home office. What strikes people as odd for a company that works exclusively with developing church facilities is that the church in the picture is boarded up and obviously no longer in use. But it was purposely hung there to serve as a reminder to us and a testimony to all who visit that everything we do is about the ministry, not about the building.

The church in the picture is the one where my grandfather, who in his mid-20s, came to know the Lord. Before that, Grandpa didn't pretend to be a Christian nor did he necessarily care to associate with those who were. And he certainly didn't want to go to church, until – through the persistence of my great-grandmother – he consented to attend a midweek revival service. He agreed to go a second night, and God changed his heart and his life. Grandpa moved his family to the other side of the tracks to get out of debt. Then he left coal mining and the sale of household products to go into the ministry.

That monumental decision has had a significant influence on our family and an untold number of other families for more than three generations. The influence of the ministry of that little country church has subsequently influenced many people for eternity. And that influence will continue to affect future generations for as long as the Lord tarries. The building is boarded up and awaiting demolition, but the influence of the ministry will continue forever.

In worship, it is the person who is significant, not the place. Jesus is our example of this in that he visited the synagogues but did not limit his fellowship to the building. The scriptures make it clear that the people are the temples where God dwells, not the physical buildings. The buildings are tools to be used for worship, Christian education, prayer and fellowship. The buildings can be consecrated to God, but he no more dwells in the carpet or the concrete or the wood than he does in the church van or hymnal or a video projector.

THE BUILDING AS A TOOL

So who is right? Is it the congregations that would build simple multipurpose structures void of symbolism, or those who say the sanctuary should be lofty and beautiful and rich with symbolism and heritage? The reality is that both are right, as are many other congregations who have different ideas about what a worship building should look like.

It is important to remember the building is a tool for ministry. The building is not sacred; what is sacred is the ministry – the worship, education and fellowship – all the activities that happen in and around and because of the building.

Since the building is a tool, it is important to step back and release all preconceived ideas about what the building should be and focus on what you believe God would have for the ministry of your church. Don't simply move in a direction because that is what you have done in the past or because that is what a church in your denomination or your area recently tried. Understand who your church is in the context of your denomination, location and history, and determine where you are headed. Decisions about symbolism, liturgy, aesthetics, sizes and shapes of rooms, and appearance to the community should be made purposefully and intentionally to move your congregation in the direction that you have determined God would have you go. When you are preparing to develop facilities (tools for your ministry), you have the opportunity to shape them to serve you. Once the facilities are erected, to a large degree, they will shape how you carry out your ministries.

The prospect of a building program represents a tremendous stewardship responsibility. God calls us to be stewards of the resources he has given. A building program usually represents the largest expenditure of those resources, so it is incumbent on us to be wise and resolute in the development of the facilities. God holds us accountable for the utilization of those resources.

This is not meant to minimize the role of buildings in the life of a church. It is meant to put them in their proper perspective. We must honor God in all we do. So many resources (time, effort and dollars) go into a building program that it all too often is seen as an end and not a means. A building program is a weighty proposition for almost any congregation, and it shouldn't be undertaken unless there is no other viable way to move your ministry forward.

If you do move ahead, it is my hope and prayer that this book will be a helpful guide.

DEFINITION OF SUCCESS

This book was compiled from the insights I have developed in over 20 years of serving churches and building programs. While there are certain paths I believe improve your chances for success, there is not one path that guarantees success. This will provide you with an overall guide, but ultimately, God is the real authority. Every dream, every schematic design, every block and every board must be committed to God in prayer. God provides the wisdom (James 1:5-6), gives the direction (Proverbs 3:5-6), sustains (Psalms 18:35), and ultimately accomplishes all (Ephesians 3:20-21).

I don't want to presume to tell you what is right for you to believe about the specific role of facilities in your ministry. You may call the part of the church used for corporate worship the sanctuary or nave or worship center or auditorium or some other name. Any of them can be right. What is important is that you know and understand the ministry direction God desires for your church.

Are you committed to doing what is best to accomplish the ministry direction? Are you willing to explore alternatives to a building program that may be more effective and less costly?

There is no approach that fits everyone, but there do seem to be general trends that can serve most situations. Over the past several years, many more churches are moving to facilities that can be used in a variety of ways. The trend involves designing and building facilities that can accommodate multiple functions.

Another trend is a greater integration of the technological capabilities for audio, video and special effects. Churches are making use of the technologies available today to communicate the gospel and promote discipleship.

Another significant trend is toward multiple ministry venues. Many churches are reaching into their communities with coffee shops, cafes and gathering places we would not immediately recognize as being a church. They may project the service from the main campus on a screen in one of these alternate venues. The service may be live or videotaped. Either way, it can provide an entry point for someone who might not initially set foot in a traditional church building.

The other question to ask yourself is, "what is the real barrier to our growth?" There are times when a church looks to a building program to solve the need without clearly understanding the need itself. A church's barrier to growth may be lack of staff. Maybe the church doesn't have a clear mission.

You must discover what the correct ministry direction is for your church. If it involves a building program, I can give you a broad understanding of the processes involved so that you can make the most effective decisions. I trust this book will provide you insights in the critical aspects of planning, preparation, committee structure and leadership that will help you achieve a successful building program.

It is not likely that your project will be a disaster. What you want to do, though, is maximize the value of the resources that will be invested in this project. It is important to recognize that those resources are not just the dollars that are spent throughout the physical construction of the building. Those resources also include an investment of time and energy on the part of the leadership and pastoral staff. The other potential cost is to the ministry itself. The cost of lost ministry during the program is the time and energy taken away from ministries. But the cost of an ill-suited facility that is unable to adequately meet future ministry needs is astronomical. The whole reason of the building is to meet ministry needs. If it doesn't do that well, it may not have been wise to spend the money at all. There are also future operational maintenance costs of the building that initially seem small but will have a profound effect throughout the life of the building. The key to a successful building program is to maximize the value in the expense of those resources.

A successful building program results in the construction and/ or renovation of the facilities that best meet a purposeful, comprehensive ministry plan and financial plan. A successful project can be identified by at least five characteristics:

1.   A clear understanding of the mission of the church. How are you serving your community? Who are you reaching outside the church walls? How are you ministering to the body of Christ?

2.   A clear understanding of the needs that are to be met after the development of the new facility, and there is no other way to accomplish these needs without a building program.

3.   A budget for the building program that takes into account all current and future aspects of the church including the staff, ministry materials and missions.

4.   A general sense of unity throughout the church on the building program because the leaders understand the ministry direction of the church and how this facility will help them meet those needs.

5.   Erecting a facility that is as pain-free as possible so that the church has the energy to hit the ground running when it moves into the facility.

This is where the analogy of climbing a mountain breaks down. In climbing, it is the exhilaration of the climb itself and the invigorating feel of getting to the summit. Then you get back down, and it is over. But a church cannot afford to sit back and relax when the building program is over. The purpose of the church is ministry in whatever emphasis characterizes your approach to the mission God has given you.

The final characteristic of a successful building program is one that allows the church to focus on the ministry throughout the building program. The building program opens the door to even greater opportunities when the program is completed. And that is more exciting than any mountain summit.

Chapter 2- Before You Begin

FRAMEWORK

The vast majority of people in leadership positions in churches throughout America have at least some knowledge of the building program process. To make best use of that knowledge, it will be helpful to construct a framework of the overall process so that we can build on it with additional insights. This framework will outline the overall process and then allow us to drill down into the specific aspects of each stage. Most building programs begin with the recognition of the need. They may sense that the ministries are being limited by the current facilities. Or perhaps there is a vision for a new ministry that cannot reach its full potential because of inadequate facilities. Once the need is thoroughly communicated and accepted by enough people in the congregation, the spark to get the ball rolling is ignited, producing the energy to make it happen.

Since there are so many aspects and approaches to conducting a building program, the first thing to do is to develop a common understanding of the elements that typically make up a building program. Each of these elements will have different nuances depending on the specific decisions you make throughout a program. This view of the overall process will allow you to plug in what you know and explain the balance of the process.

There are a number of ways to describe and outline a building process. Sometimes there are multiple words to describe the same facet. For instance, the drawings used by the subcontractors and contractors in construction can be referred to as working drawings, blueprints, construction drawings, construction documents or building plans. We want to begin with a common understanding of some of the terminology.

The framework we will use involves three aspects: Phases, Events and Activities (see Exhibit 1A). Phases will be the broad sections of a building program that are generally linear in time. The Events are the major occurrences within the Phases, and the Activities are the actions that go into making up the Events.

PHASES

We will begin by dividing the entire process into four phases. The phases will run in chronological order and, in general, the next phase will begin about the time the previous phase ends. These phases do not necessarily divide the entire process into four equal time components. In fact, their length will likely vary dramatically. There are occasions when there could be substantial time between any two of the phases, but they will not normally overlap significantly.

We start with the Preparation Phase. It encompasses the point when the church leadership has the sense that the facilities are constricting the ministry and it wants to see what changes, if any, should be made. This is when the church will begin to organize to move forward in the building program, filling key committee positions. It is time for gathering information about where you are and where you have been. This phase could overlap one of the others. There are times when a church moves into the subsequent phases and realizes there is additional preparation that needs to be done.

Next is the Planning Phase. If the Preparation Phase is looking at the past and present, the Planning Phase is when you begin to look to the future. This is when you begin to involve industry professionals, often from outside your congregation. They will help you quantify and prioritize your programming needs and begin to put them on paper in the form of preliminary designs. This is when you find out whether new or enhanced facilities are the answer to your ministry needs. Here you begin to consider building solutions to determine what it will take to meet your needs and accomplish your objectives.

The Design Phase comes third and begins when specific plans take shape and when significant dollars are invested to move ahead with construction documents, civil engineering, surveying and site testing. This is when you secure official church approvals from your denomination and/or church body to spend money to design building plans. Also needed at this time is approval from local government panels, including planning and zoning, architectural review, health, water and building boards. Everything that is required before beginning construction is completed in this phase.

The last part is the Construction Phase. This is when the contractor breaks ground. It requires input from the church to coordinate with the industry professionals to deliver what has been dreamed and designed. The end of this phase is traditionally marked by the occupancy of the new facilities and celebrating a new beginning in the life of the church.

COMMON EVENTS
IN A BUILDING PROGRAM

Six events are common to nearly all building programs: Select a Building Committee; Engage the Professionals; Design the Project; Obtain the Funding; Construct the Project; and Celebrate the Completion. Select the Building Committee is the first event, and it occurs in the PREPARATION PHASE. For the time being, we will use this as an all-encompassing term referring to all the committees engaged for the building program. It nearly always involves two committees: building and finance. Depending, however, on the denomination, the building committee could be just the pastor and his staff. For large churches, I have seen multiple committees that might include building, finance, communication, colors, sound and video, furnishings, site development, construction development and others.

Whatever its size and makeup, the building committee will be responsible for the administration of the project. It will engage the professionals and work with them to design and build the facilities. It is also responsible for communication throughout the project to the church leadership, the congregation and the community. This committee is typically responsible for obtaining any church approvals necessary as dictated by the specific church government. Some organizations don't require congregational approval, but getting a vote of confidence from the church body is still a good idea.

The next event is to Engage the Professionals. It occurs in the PLANNING PHASE. This refers to all industry professionals who will play a role in the project. The way their services are engaged can vary widely on what is typically referred to as the "project delivery system." For instance, one project delivery system would be contracting with an architect, putting it out to bid and then selecting a contractor from among the low bidders.

Another project delivery system might be bringing the architect and contractor together from the beginning in a design-build approach. Some churches may consider serving as their own general contractor. These and other project delivery systems will be discussed in more detail in Chapter 6.

The first common event in the DESIGN PHASE is to Design the Project. In the PLANNING PHASE the building committee selected a project delivery method and engaged the key industry professionals to lead them through the design of the project. Some of the early steps in the design process could be considered part of the PLANNING PHASE. In that phase, the design professionals will have worked with the building committee to develop a need and desire summary of what the project could accomplish. This programming statement is often a narrative that puts the building committee and design professionals on the same page by outlining the direction the design will take.

After programming, the entire design process can be divided into four parts.

- Preliminary/schematic design: the early stages of the design where you work back and forth to plan the project.

- Design development: A preliminary design is further refined for code implications and site characteristics.

- Construction documents: They serve as the drawings that will be used to secure permits and construct the actual facility.

- Construction administration: assistance through the construction phase. It also includes the civil engineering and site design to develop the property. We will look at these in more detail in Chapter 7.

At the end of the Design the Project event, there will be a need to Procure the Permits. This is becoming a more and more significant part of the overall building process as regulations are skyrocketing, particularly in densely populated and coastal regions. There are still some areas of the country where minimal documentation is needed to obtain a building permit, but that is now the exception to the rule. More often, site development approvals are required, which can lead to lengthy processes involving water management, utility tie-ins, parking, site lighting and setbacks. It may be necessary to get variances for relief, for instance, on parking or height requirements, which will necessitate another approval process. There also may be the need to re-zone a property in a separate process. Sometimes approvals by separate architectural review committees are required, especially in historical districts. Your industry professional should be able to help you navigate this web of approvals to go on with construction.

Perhaps the single most common event is the necessity to Obtain Funding. It may simply be done for cash or involve a more complex loan arrangement, but whatever the project is, it will require funds (in the DESIGN PHASE before construction can begin). The most common arrangement typically includes a combination of cash and conventional financing. But there are other approaches. Another factor is the fund-raising program that could be done in-house or through a company that specialize in capital stewardship campaigns. You may have a mandate to build for cash or be willing to explore an unconventional approach to financing. Either way, funds will be necessary. We will outline some of the approaches in Chapters 5 and 8.

The CONSTRUCTION PHASE is obviously where you Construct the Project. The specific activities that the church will undertake in this are largely dependent on the project delivery method selected and the role of the industry professionals. During this phase, a financial system will need to be set up to account for and approve invoices as the construction progresses. There also needs to be a process to handle adjustments requested or required during construction. Normally, a thorough job in early phases will help to avoid excessive adjustments throughout construction. Quality work in the earlier phases determines the overall success of the project, since the CONSTRUCTION PHASE is simply carrying out what has been dictated.

The final event in the CONSTRUCTION PHASE and in the entire process is to Celebrate the Completion. This is the point at which you occupy the new facility and begin to use it as intended. This is also normally referred to as the dedication or consecration. It is a celebration because it represents the culmination of the efforts of many people. It is the physical manifestation of the dreams of those who have sacrificed time and money. It is a time worthy of celebration.

PROJECT CONTROL TIME LINE

The focus of a building program tends to always fall on the CONSTRUCTION PHASE. That is understandable because of the investment of many hours and meetings over months of planning and then seemingly endless weeks of permitting, where you wondered, at times, if anything was moving forward. As the facility comes out of the ground, the excitement and anticipation reach a peak as the congregation begins to see the reality of what it has heard about, pledged toward and dreamed of. It is also when the vast majority of the dollars are expended, usually about 90 percent of the cost of the entire process.

The focus on the CONSTRUCTION PHASE may be understandable, but it is somewhat misplaced. By the time you reach the construction phase, the project itself is essentially set in stone. During construction, the industry professionals are constructing what has already been determined. Unless there is a major challenge that forces significant changes on the project, the only adjustments to the building will be relatively minor. To

Exhibit 2A

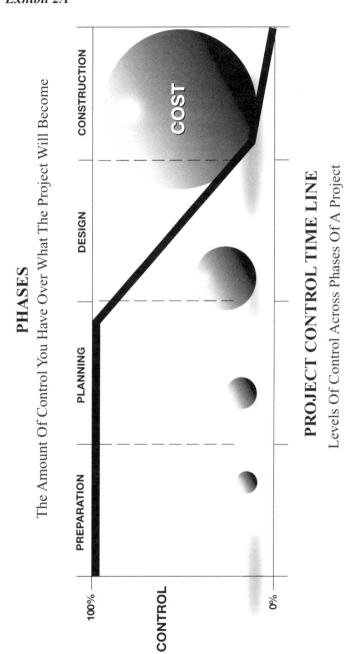

PHASES

The Amount Of Control You Have Over What The Project Will Become

PREPARATION · PLANNING · DESIGN · CONSTRUCTION

CONTROL · 100% · 0%

COST

PROJECT CONTROL TIME LINE

Levels Of Control Across Phases Of A Project

a great extent, the church is locked in to what the project will be long before the CONSTRUCTION PHASE begins.

Consider the time line in Exhibit 2A. This time line graphically depicts the amount of control you have over the nature, scope, focus and quality of the project. It doesn't mean that the project could not be abandoned or dramatically changed in its latter stages. The reality is you won't. The congregation becomes invested financially and emotionally in what it will be getting with this new facility. As that investment grows, it becomes increasingly difficult to change course, even if you're currently on the wrong one. Therefore, the focus should be on the earlier phases.

I visited a pastor who had recently finished a relocation project with another firm. During our visit, he recounted his experience. The church hired an architectural firm that it believed would provide creativity and a high profile design. Unfortunately, the church focused on the exterior appearance of the facility, while the functions of the building became an afterthought. The pastor knew they were on track for a building they couldn't afford and one that wouldn't effectively meet their needs. But it was a captivating picture of what the church could look like, and the committee was sold. The congregation embraced the design, which added to the agony when the pastor's fears were realized. The project had to be redesigned, which cost time and even more money. Even the redesign ended up 15 percent over-budget, and all because it was too difficult to shift the momentum that had developed early on.

At the beginning of the project and throughout the PREPARATION PHASE you have total control over where you want to go with the building program. Gather information and assess needs early in the process. You have complete freedom to decide the size, type and location of the facility. You can still easily consider relocation or not building at all.

In the PLANNING PHASE you begin to think in general of the type of facility you might need to address the ministry needs. You are beginning to work now with the industry professionals to develop a program of needs and wants, and you are beginning to discuss the type of facility that might be best for the ministry of the church. Things begin to take shape a little bit here, but you still have tremendous flexibility with what you want to do since nothing has been shown to the congregation and there has been only a relatively minor financial investment thus far.

Then you encounter the DESIGN PHASE. This is where the direction of the facility is determined. In the early part of the DESIGN PHASE you are reviewing preliminary drawings in a process where each new drawing further develops the scope of the facility. At some point you feel comfortable enough to show preliminary drawings to the congregation, which begins to buy into the direction. Upon agreement of the preliminary drawings, you authorize the design professionals to go ahead with the construction documents. At this time, you are probably committing the largest amount of funds to date and you have decided the scope, type of facility and level of quality. Now your flexibility of control is diminished greatly.

While the majority of the dollars are spent during the CONSTRUCTION PHASE, it is the DESIGN PHASE that determines the scope of the dollars to be spent. During the CONSTRUCTION PHASE you can save some dollars by deciding to adjust the finishes or get a better deal on windows. But there is relatively little that you can do by then (short of a major overhaul and redesign) to save money. The largest amount of dollars to be saved does not occur in the CONSTRUCTION PHASE. Potentially, the project could fluctuate by a few thousands of dollars in the CONSTRUCTION PHASE, but tens of thousands and even hundreds of thousands of dollars will be saved or spent in the PLANNING and DESIGN PHASES.

NOT-SO-COMMON EVENTS
IN A BUILDING PROGRAM

Here is how to make the DESIGN PHASE successful. The DESIGN PHASE will be successful in matching the facility to your ministry needs and budget if some additional steps are taken in the PREPARATION and PLANNING PHASES. That leads us to the not-so-common events in a building program.

There are four events that are too often overlooked or taken for granted. They may be seen as unnecessary because the church does not understand the impact they have on determining the success of the project, or they simply may not have occurred to the church to carry out these events. The administration or exclusion of them will affect, positively or negatively, the success of the project.

The first not-so-common event occurs in the PREPARATION PHASE. It is key to Understand Who You Are. At first glance this seems overly simplistic. Perhaps you have attended the church for decades – of course you know who the church is. But do you really? Do you know what trends have taken place in the demographics of your congregation and how they compare with other churches in your denomination or surrounding area? Do you know what population shifts are going on in your community? Do you know what goes through the mind of a first-time visitor? It is important to know the answers to these and other questions to truly know who you are. Chapter 3 has been committed to discussing this issue.

Understanding who you are is also important when you Plan the Ministry Direction, another not-so-common event in the PREPARATION PHASE. Once you really know who you are in the context of your community and what you believe God desires for your church, then you can begin to plan the ministry direction. You can evaluate your current ministries to see whether they are maximizing their potential. You determine what ministries are integral to the mission of the church and what new ministries should be added. It is a proactive process to understand where ministry opportunities exist. This is the step where the church purposely stops to understand from God exactly what their ministry should be. Hopefully, it is a time to think outside the box and not just blindly continue to do things because that is the way you have always done them. You may very well end up with similar ministry goals, but it will be an understanding that brings you greater resolve and commitment. We will go into more detail in Chapter 3.

The next not-so-common event that occurs in the PREPARATION PHASE is to Establish the Budget. I've learned that this is the one misstep that is responsible for the majority of church construction disasters. Some churches take the approach that this is not necessary since they will just design and build what they believe God wants them to do, and he will provide the money. I certainly have no dispute that God can provide in a miraculous way, but I believe most of the time he chooses to work through his people. Budgeting is an assessment of where you are financially and determining what you will spend for the building program. We will discuss this more thoroughly in Chapter 5.

The last not-so-common event that arguably occurs most often in the PLANNING PHASE is to Develop a Master Plan. A master plan is an overall site plan of development that maximizes the ministry possibilities of a church's entire property. It seeks to balance worship, education, fellowship and parking when the entire site is developed. It is a living document that is to be revisited and revised with changes in a given church's ministry direction. It can be overlooked as unnecessary "because we are just planning to add some educational expansions, so we will just put it here." However, by first looking at the master plan possibilities, the church may find that the best location for that educational facility is different than originally planned. The master plan can save money by enlightening a church as to what it could do in a current phase that could help down the road.

An important activity that should occur in this event is to Investigate Site Specific Issues. This is something that ultimately happens, if not purposely then by default. There are times when church projects go all the way through planning and design and begin the permitting process. Then they find out they are in an area that is not zoned for churches, and the re-zoning process can set the project back for months. Had the church and the industry professionals conducted a code investigation in the PLANNING PHASE, then they could have started the re-zoning process with the PLANNING and DESIGN PHASES so that no time was lost. Today, wetland restrictions are a common issue that must be investigated so that you are aware of the exact amount of your property that can be used. Sometimes the building can be designed in violation of setback or height requirements. If those are not determined until the permitting event, there can be considerable costs and time lost to make the adjustments. When the code investigation is done in the PLANNING PHASE, it will improve the integrity of the preliminary design and eliminate most surprises that could hit a church in the DESIGN and CONSTRUCTION PHASES. We will look at all these issues in more detail in Chapter 7.

The last event to consider has, in part, been mentioned. In the Common Events in a Building Program, Celebrate the Completion was discussed. It was referred by that name because that is what most congregations do. They celebrate the completion of the building program. I agree it is an appropriate time to celebrate, but I would suggest celebrating the beginning. The end of construction is not really an ending, but rather a beginning. The whole purpose for the building was to build the impact of the ministry. It seems to me that should be the focus of the celebration.

Exhibit 2B

PREPARATION PHASE

UNDERSTAND WHO YOU ARE
- Review Your History
- Analyze Your Surroundings
- Take a Look Inside

PLAN THE MINISTRY DIRECTION
- Develop the Mission
- Determine the Strategic Priorities
- Assemble Pertinent Data

SELECT THE BUILDING COMMITTEE
- Select the People
- Decide on the Structure
- Plan Committee Activities

PLANNING PHASE

ESTABLISH THE BUDGET
- Investigate Funding Alternatives
- Establish Financial Parameters
- Decide on Capital Stewardship Campaign

ENGAGE INDUSTRY PROFESSIONALS
- Identify Industry Professionals
- Understand Project Delivery Methods
- Know Your Contract

DEVELOP A MASTER PLAN
- Develop a Program Statement
- Investigate Site Specific Issues
- Do Preliminary Design

EVENTS IN A

DESIGN
PHASE

CONSTRUCTION
PHASE

DESIGN THE PROJECT
• Finish Design Development
• Produce Construction
  Documents
• Procure Permits

OBTAIN FUNDING
• Select Funding Approach
• Prepare Financial Packages

CONSTRUCT THE PROJECT

CELEBRATE THE BEGINNING

BUILDING PROGRAM

ACTIVITIES

There are several activities that will take place under events mentioned above. These activities are accomplished to achieve a positive outcome in each event. The success of these events in the first three phases determines the success of the overall project. Some of events such as Procure the Permits and Investigate Site Specific Issues have already been mentioned.

To understand who you are, the steps will be to Review Your History, Analyze Your Surroundings and Take a Look Inside. This understanding then forms the foundation for you to be able to Plan the Ministry Direction. These steps include Developing the Mission and then Determining the Strategic Priorities to accomplish the mission. It also includes Assembling the Pertinent Data to go forward into your building program.

The Selection of the Building Committee is an important event because it involves the individuals who will communicate the mission to the industry professionals and administer the next three phases. For that to be successful, it is important to make the right Selection of People and leadership of the committee. The leadership of the church must Decide on the Structure of the committees and subcommittees that best fits the leadership capabilities and opportunities presented by the building program. The people selected can Plan the Committee Activities that are described in the next two phases but also include communication and securing church approvals.

To Establish the Budget, you must Establish Financial Parameters that will become the guidelines for the project. A Decision on a Capital Stewardship Campaign is pivotal because that can have an impact on the financial parameters. The committee must also do an early Investigation of Funding Alternatives to put together the financial plan.

The committee will Engage Industry Professionals to form the balance of the team that, along with the building committee, will lead the building program. The first step in engaging industry professionals will be Identify the Industry Professionals that will be necessary for your project. Then you must Understand the Project Delivery Methods to be able to decide on what method best fits your needs. Then you must Know Your Contract to avoid costly mistakes due to misunderstandings and disputes.

After the industry professionals are engaged, they will work with the building committee to Develop a Master Plan. They will Conduct the Strategic Investigation mentioned above to understand the opportunities and limitations of the site. They will work with the building committee to understand the ministry direction and the building needs identified by the ministry direction and Develop a Program Statement that, in general, would address those needs. They will then Do Preliminary Design work, which begins to put lines on paper outlining what was developed in the program statement with an eye on the budget.

When the preliminary work is completed and the industry professionals move into Completing Design Development, you will then enter DESIGN PHASE. The industry professionals will then Produce the Construction Documents that will be used to Procure the Permits and complete the facility.

During the DESIGN PHASE it will also be necessary to Obtain the Funding. To obtain the funding, the committee will Select the Funding Approach that best meets the needs of the church. They will then Prepare a Financial Package that will be used by the lending institutions to make their final evaluation before providing the funds.

These are the specific Activities that make up the Events, which occur within logical PHASES in the building process. This is the framework we will use to explore in the following chapters what it takes to achieve a successful building program.

Before You Build
Chapter 3- Before You Plan

UNDERSTAND WHO YOU ARE
• Review Your History
• Analyze Your Surroundings
• Take a Look Inside

PLAN THE MINISTRY DIRECTION
• Develop the Mission
• Determine the Strategic Priorities
• Assemble Pertinent Data

The PREPARATION PHASE is by far the most overlooked and under-utilized phase of the building process. Many churches jump into the process selecting a building committee to begin a design on what they assume to be the appropriate direction without a full understanding of their needs. I worked with a church that was aware of a pressing need for fellowship space and was so focused on trying to meet that need that it failed to recognize it also had deficiencies in educational and worship facilities. Looking more closely at their mission, property and finances, church leaders were able to develop a plan that addressed all those needs. Taking the time to see the big picture was crucial to bringing about a desired result.

In other situations, church leaders may discover that building a new facility is not the right approach. Sometimes the best thing a church can do to make better use of the facilities is to renovate. In other cases, it may mean an expansion that would require relocation or purchase of additional property. Part of the answer to a church's needs will involve non-building issues such as staff, ministries, leadership and missions.

It is very difficult to know the right direction without a complete understanding of where the ministry is headed. Spending time reviewing where you have come from and analyzing the community that surrounds you can provide understanding and context to form a foundation for decisions regarding future ministries and facilities.

KNOW YOUR PAST

The first step to Understand Who You Are is to Review Your History. A review of your church's history is not an idle exercise for the historical committee. As Abraham Lincoln stated, "If we could first know where we are, and whether we are tending, we could then better judge what to do, and how to do it." An understanding of where the church has been will help you preserve the part of your heritage that is integral to your faith and the gospel yet allow you to eliminate outdated methods. You want to be able to separate the cultural from the eternal, so the eternal can be protected at all costs and the cultural can be adjusted to meet your ministry needs.

Zig Zigler, motivational speaker and bestselling author, tells the story of how his wife always cut off the end of a ham before she put it into the oven to be cooked. Her only explanation was that her mother did it. At a family reunion, they had the opportunity to speak with his wife's mother, who said that she cut off the end of the ham because that is what her mother did. When the grandmother was asked about it, she said she cut off the end of the ham to get it to fit into her oven. A review of your history will help you better understand why your church does what it does. It will help you embrace the activities that are vital and give up those that are essentially "cutting off the end of the ham."

That review, if you are part of a denomination, will include a look at the heritage of that denomination. Virtually every denomination started out of burning passions and desires that men and women believed were from God. Many denominations have evolved significantly, for better or for worse, from their roots. You might be surprised at the thoughts and beliefs of your founders. If you are part of a denomination, this background will be beneficial. Sift through the treasures of your history for the distinctions of eternal consequence.

Look at the names traditionally used for church facilities – parish hall, fellowship hall, family life center and gymnasium. Do you use a split chancel or a central pulpit? Is it an altar or communion table? Is it centered below and in front or raised and near the back? Do you use an altar rail or mourners bench? Is the choir at the back of the chancel or to the side? Or is it hidden behind a screen or in a loft at the rear of the sanctuary? Understanding the answers to these questions will help you understand what part of your heritage should be retained and what part needs to be adjusted as times have changed.

You will also want to look at the characteristics of your church. How long have you been in existence? Has it been a transient church or made up of families for generations? What has been the socioeconomic evolution of the church? What has been the track record for worship attendance, Christian education and fellowship? Has the ratio among these ministries remained constant? Denominational headquarters should be able to help pull together historical and statistical data.

LOOK AROUND

The next activity is to Analyze Your Surroundings. Look to your geographic region, then to your community, then to your neighborhood for insights into the socioeconomic makeup of the people who comprise your ministry potential. Without understanding the subtle yet significant shifts that are taking place, you can move ahead with assumptions and perspectives very different from reality. This information can help to explain areas of success you may be currently realizing and show you where you can build on these strengths. They also may make you aware of needs that are not being met.

We all tend to travel in specific social circles. We frequent certain restaurants, shop at certain stores, attend various social events and usually attend a single church. We see familiar faces and share in one another's lives to varying degrees. We tend to get our news from the same newspapers, radio programs, Web sites and television networks. We feel like we see a lot of the world and assume we have a broad base from which to form our perceptions of what is going on globally, nationally and locally.

That was the way my dad described his perception of the community he had been living in since 1957. A series of events in 1987 led him to begin a weekly ministry in a bar he had never previously entered. That outreach and the subsequent compassionate ministries that have flourished since then made Dad aware of how limited his perspective was of the community he thought he knew so well. Reviewing demographic information gives church leaders a chance to see whether the traditional understanding of your community matches the realities taking place there.

The U.S. Census Bureau breaks down the population in communities by age, marital status, numbers in households, income and occupation. Other sources of demographic information include state and local Chambers of Commerce, state and local employment offices, local school census data and federal agencies.

There are some sources that specialize in taking the demographics a step further, providing the information in a form that can be more meaningful to a church. They identify, compare and contrast life-styles in a community and then analyze the data to provide statistics about religious preferences, key value, primary concerns, racial and ethnic diversity, family structure and education. This kind of analysis can make a church aware of new opportunities for ministry.

INTROSPECTION

The third activity is to Take a Look Inside. Doing that requires looking at your own demographics. What is the age breakdown of the congregation? How far do they drive? How does a life-style analysis compare with the surrounding community? What trends do we see in the growth? Is the growth coming from specific demographic, geographic or economic areas?

Another part of looking inside is to review your financial situation. What is the trend in overall giving? How do your expenses break down among staff, supplies, facilities and other needs? What is your financial five-year trend?

The third part of looking inside involves getting someone to look inside for you. After you attend a church week after week, year after year, there is a tendency to not notice the peeling paint or the wrinkle in the carpet or the convoluted way of getting from the narthex to the nursery and back to the worship center.

It is important to take a fresh look so that you can understand the impressions of a first-time visitor. Find out from visitors who became regulars what attracted them initially and then became their reason they continued to attend. They can also give you insights into things they didn't like but were willing to overlook. Visitors who did not stay also can be a valuable source of information. If they can be made to feel at ease and open, they can provide excellent input. Be careful not to prejudge the people in an effort to reason away information that might be difficult to hear.

Another facet of this fresh look is to understand the community's perceptions of your church. This insight will help you launch new ministry initiatives by knowing more fully how the community will receive them. Some of this information might be painful, but it could help to clarify incorrect perceptions and open opportunities for outreach right in your back yard.

A simple option for getting a fresh look would be to have friends from another church visit who would be willing to be brutally honest about what they encounter. Ask them to evaluate everything from the approach and appearance of the facilities, the way they were greeted, the general tone of the congregation, interior impressions, the teaching and the worship.

Perhaps the best step would be to contract with a consultant who specializes in reviewing these matters. There are firms that are excellent in analyzing the current situation of a church. They will evaluate what you are doing in context of your community and your mission. They can help identify the barriers to growth, whether they are staff, parking, facilities, ministries or some combination.

ORGANIZE THE INFORMATION

Once you're done gathering information, organize it to help you to analyze and clarify your identity, strengths, opportunities and direction. A pastor friend of mine refers to discovering your identity as "finding your front door." What attracts people to visit? Why do they stay? What is your church known for in the community? What has been your focus? What makes you unique from every other church in town? What aspects of doctrine and faith are critical to what you believe? What cannot be compromised in who you are?

Peter Drucker, has been quoted as saying, "A business is not defined by the company's name, statutes or articles of incorporation. It is defined by the want the customer satisfies when he buys a product or service. The question, 'What is our business?' can, therefore, be answered only by looking at the business from the outside, from the point of view of the customer, and the market."[1]

That could be paraphrased for churches by saying, "A church is not defined by its name, statutes or articles of incorporation. It is defined by the need that is satisfied when a person comes in contact with the church. The question, 'What is our mission?' can, therefore, be answered only by looking at the ministry from the outside, from the point of view of the people being served." Ministry doesn't take place until lives have been effectively touched.

Looking at your strengths is nothing more than identifying what your church does well. Identifying opportunities means building on your strengths. For instance, a strong children's ministry might be the impetus to offering practical outreach services in the areas of parenting skills, family budgeting and managing households.

The final step is to determine where you are going. A clear sense of direction can be a catalyst and a road map. Bob Biehl, author of "Master Planning," lists these benefits of a clear plan:

1. Increases team spirit because everyone plays off the same sheet of music;

2. Increases framework clarity required for growing the organization, solving problems, orienting staff, communicating effectively, and making wise decisions;

3. Reduces organizational frustration, tension and pressure by putting assumptions in writing.[2]

MOVE FORWARD

The first step is to establish your beliefs. These are your foundational, unchanging and unwavering tenants of faith that will not change with time or circumstances. They will obviously reflect your doctrinal background. These are the ideas and beliefs that form the foundation of the institution and are the things that you will never give up. You have spent time researching history of your church and, if appropriate, your denomination. You found those elements of faith along with the scriptures that must not change in 10 years, 100 years or 1,000 years. The beliefs will form the context from which everything else will operate.

The mission statement answers the question, "Why do we exist?" It will describe why you do what you do and not how you do it. It should be short, focused and easily understood. I have heard it said that it should be something that could fit on a T-shirt or be able to be repeated by a 10-year-old or something you should be able to cite at gunpoint. It is a statement that proclaims, "This is why we are here." It will likely distinguish you from other churches in your neighborhood and city. Your mission statement doesn't pass judgment on those other churches. It simply acknowledges who you are as a church.

Mr. Drucker offers guidance from his book *Managing the Non-Profit Organization*: "A mission statement has to be operational; otherwise it is just good intentions. A mission statement has to focus on what the institution really tries to do and then do it so that everybody in the organization can say, this is my contribution to the goal."

The mission statement may go through drafts and revisions until the leadership is unified in the belief that it describes why your church exists. It should reflect the passion of the church. The mission statement is something that will rarely change and will likely be part of the heart of the church for years to come. If the church accomplishes the mission, it succeeds. If it does not, it fails.

The next step is to establish the objectives. Objectives are what are necessary to move the church forward toward completing its mission. The objectives will be broad directions that address all facets of the mission. It is important for you to develop as many objectives as possible. The collective attainment of these objectives would mean thorough accomplishment of the mission.

Be sure to involve a number of key people in these discussions. The more input you have from informed people who are passionate about the church, the more comprehensive the planning will be. For instance, we did an exercise once where we had about approximately 30 people sitting at six tables. We were all asked to write down the name of every green vegetable we could think of. When we got through, we were then to combine our answers with those at our table, and then we looked at the results. What we found was that no one person at any table had all the answers.

A helpful tool in this process is to move beyond traditional linear thought or "vertical thinking." Vertical thinking is the process where each step builds on itself. It is the essence of mathematics and sciences. In vertical thinking, each step must be correct in and of itself and moves the process toward the solution with each step. This is the process of thought that is common for most of us and is the way we've been taught to solve problems.

Horizontal, or "lateral thinking," develops ideas for the sake of the idea and not necessarily to build logical steps directly toward a solution. Lateral thinking involves new ways of looking at things and considers alternatives even when an initial solution is found. Lateral thinking considers all alternatives no matter how unreasonable or unrealistic they sound at first. It is what is commonly referred to as "thinking outside the box." Ideas may be like a structural system in a building where the individual parts are meaningless until they are fit together to form an entire structure. They have value and integrity only as they are considered together. A lateral idea may seem to have no value until it is put together with other lateral ideas.

Passion should play a part in identifying objectives. Without a deep, burning desire to reach objectives, it is unlikely they will be anything more than words on a page. Bob Biehl suggests asking yourself, "What makes me weep or pound the table?"

While objectives are general directions, goals need to be specific. For instance, an objective may be to have a comprehensive youth program where one of the goals may be to have 20 elementary age pupils in Bible quizzing. The goals may require stretching and growing but not so far out that they become demotivating. They need to be relevant in that they must support the objective. And they must be time bound so that there is a time frame to evaluate when the goal is accomplished.

Goals can range anywhere from one to 10 years. And some complex goals will have several facets. It may be advantageous to divide them up into short term and long term. Generally, the short-term goals will be more specific and will support the long-term goals.

The most helpful way I have found to develop goals is to construct them so that they are SMART Goals. SMART Goals are made up of five distinct characteristics:

S – Specific. *It can't be misinterpreted.*
M– Measurable. *It can be measured.*
A – Achievable. *It stretches but doesn't demoralize.*
R – Relevant. *They are meaningful to the objective.*
T – Time Bound. *There is a timeframe within which the goal will be accomplished.*

The final step in the strategic ministry plan outline is the strategy. This is the step where resources are identified and allocated. This is where resources get allocated for the tools to accomplish the goals to meet the objective to accomplish the mission.

Strategy bridges the gap created by "where we are headed" and "where we want to go." Strategy deals with specific action programs, who will perform them and when. These specifics allocate and focus resources in the right direction. Strategy also fits the controls to specific management needs so that the church is always aware of the progress toward or deviation from the objectives.

I cannot underestimate the importance of prayer in any part of this process, but especially with strategic ministry plan, which is essentially determining what God wants you to do as a church. Saturate that work with prayer.

WHAT'S IMPORTANT NOW?

Once strategies are established, you need to Determine the Strategic Priorities. The question to ask is, "What is most important now?" This is the question many churches want to start with before taking time to develop a strategic ministry plan. With the understandings that come from developing a strategic ministry plan, you can answer this question with credibility and confidence. What staff, volunteers, materials, facilities and other resources will be needed as part of the strategy?

This strategic planning stimulates the future by reallocating resources to what is vital. And it focuses the key elements of the church on the main issues, avoiding wasting time and energy on peripheral issues and becoming a victim of the mistaken idea that activity (being busy) equals success. It enables the church to stay focused so that it is not lulled to sleep, even by successes.

Until now we have not concerned ourselves with buildings. We have been working specifically to identify and understand the ministries of the church and how to carry them out. Now we begin to explore whether new or renovated facilities are necessary to accomplish the mission. If you have come to this point and new facilities are not required, then there is no need for the balance of this book with the possible exception of long-range financial planning.

However, if you find that new facilities will be required to accomplish your mission, it's time to assemble the following pertinent data before moving on to the next steps in the process:

1. Strategic ministry plan outline
2. Church history
3. Church demographics
4. Community and life-style analysis
5. Drawings of current facilities
6. Deeds and surveys of current site
7. Financial documents

[1] Peter Drucker. *The Essential Drucker. New York, NY. HarperCollins Publishers, Inc. 2001*

[2] *Bob Biehl. Master Planning. Nashville, TN. Broadman*

Before You Build
Chapter 4- Before You Select the
Building Committee

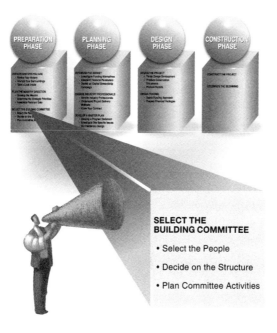

**SELECT THE
BUILDING COMMITTEE**

• Select the People

• Decide on the Structure

• Plan Committee Activities

The process of the development of the physical church facilities is part of the overall ongoing life of most churches. The building program is only a snapshot in the life of the church and, therefore, should never be viewed as an end but rather the means of providing a valuable tool for the ongoing ministry of the church. If you look at the time line of the life of the church, the erection of facilities is just a point in time where tools were acquired to do additional ministry. It is much like acquiring other tools such as a computer or sound system or church bus, except that, given the impact on the church's financial and other resources, building facilities will have a much greater positive or negative impact on the life of the church.

The work of introspection and strategic ministry planning described in Chapter 3 is not generally thought of as part of the role of the building committee. There can be an overlap in the people involved, but the purposes of the two committees are dramatically different. One committee has a very broad, all-encompassing role in determining the direction and priorities for the entire church. The other is charged with developing facilities to accomplish stated goals and objectives.

The committee that handles the work described in Chapter 3 can generally be referred to as the long-range planning committee. The distinct role of the long-range planning committee is that it is primarily concerned with the ministries of the church – where they are and where they need to be. As the committee identifies where the church is headed, it will logically determine the resource needs to accomplish the ministries. It may identify the need of new and/or renovated facilities to accomplish the mission of the church, but that is not its focus.

When the strategic ministry plan is completed and new facilities are identified as a priority, then the building committee can be assembled. It is the charge of the building committee to develop the facilities that will best assist in achieving the strategic ministry plan, both in terms of the physical facilities and the overall financial plan of the church.

The initiation and constitution of both the long-range planning and building committees originate with the leadership of the church. The leadership of your church may go by various names depending on your historical and doctrinal background. For our purposes, we will use the term leadership anytime we are referring to the governing body of the church. All other committees are initiated by and serve at the behest of the leadership.

An understanding of the strategic ministry plan is critical to the role the building committee is to play. This is leadership's responsibility. The leadership of the church must make sure that the strategic ministry plan is communicated to the building committee, and the building committee understands what is to be developed to meet the strategic ministry objectives. This can sometimes be accomplished with some overlap of personnel from the long-range planning committee and/or the leadership and the building committee. It is the responsibility of the leadership to know the building committee is on track.

WHO SHOULD SERVE?

The next activity is to select the people. Careful consideration needs to be given to the individuals who will have a significant impact in shaping the ministries to come. These people bear significant responsibility for the success of the project.

Over the years, I have worked with committees that were as few as three (the pastoral staff only) to one that was as large as 45. From my experience and from anecdotal evidence, the optimal number for a building committee is five to seven members. Most of the information put out by different denominations and independent groups tends to agree with this range.

I met with one church that I felt had an extremely large committee of approximately 25. When I spoke with the pastor the next day, he asked me to come back to meet with "the rest of the committee." We were able to get the building designed and construction to the satisfaction of nearly everyone. But it was an extremely arduous task to keep people informed of the process along the way. We had to take a lot of time at the beginning of each meeting to recap everything that had been done in prior meetings so that the people who showed up for this meeting would all be on the same page. It also took very strong leadership by the chairman to move things along when there was a tendency to discuss something that had been decided in a prior meeting.

A better use of the time and efforts of many of the people on that committee would have been to involve them on either an advisory committee or a formal committee/subcommittee of the building committee. This would allow them to perform needed legwork in their particular area of expertise or interest that would reduce some of the burden on the building committee. It would also give them a sense of ownership in what was taking place. However, for that to happen, they must feel their work is valued and their opinions are being seriously considered.

TOP 10 QUALIFICATIONS FOR BUILDING COMMITTEE MEMBERS

I'd like to present for your consideration my top 10 qualifications for building committee members, in descending order of importance. The first two qualifications must be present in every building committee member. Anything less, at its worst, is inviting potential disaster and, at its best, promises a facility that doesn't meet ministry needs. The other eight qualifications are highly recommended and may come in varying degrees in individuals.

1. Exemplary Christian life: Every building committee member should be living in such a way that earns respect both inside and outside of the church. They should be people who exhibit the fruit of the spirit. They should be able to automatically engender trust into the process simply by virtue of their participation. My initial tendency was to take this qualification for granted. Then I thought back over the building committees I have served and recognized that, sadly, this is too often not given priority. Proverbs 11:3 says, "The integrity of the upright guides them, but the unfaithful destroy by their duplicity." (NIV)

2. Thorough understanding and uncompromising support of the strategic ministry objectives of the church: This is the critical awareness that each building committee member must have to keep the project on track. They must know where the church is headed and why, and they must support that approach. Otherwise, it becomes a project of pet interests and non-critical issues that results in a facility ill-suited for where the church wants to go. They need to be able to articulate that strategic mission to industry professionals. The committee is being asked to develop facilities that, upon completion, will shape the ministry of the church. The committee's thorough understanding and uncompromising support should preclude any personal agendas and preconceived ideas.

With these two qualifications, you can develop an excellent building committee. There can be no compromises on these two qualifications. While it sounds almost too simplistic and too straightforward, it is too often not the case in many building programs.

3. Emotional intelligence: We have traditionally spoken of IQ when we think of someone's intellectual skills. In recent years it has become clear that EQ (emotional quotient) is possibly even more important than IQ in determining success. Daniel Goleman, perhaps the foremost author on this subject, describes four major components of emotional intelligence: Self-awareness, self-management, social awareness and relationship management. Emotional intelligence is having the ability to be aware of what you are feeling and then control and direct those emotions to accomplish your highest and best purpose. Along with that personal competence is the social competence of being able to understand what other people are feeling, what their concerns are and what their needs might be. Then, with that understanding, you are able to assist others in bringing out the right response.

4. Respected by the congregation: The building committee will need the support of the congregation for the program to be successful. The congregation will provide the bulk of the resources, so it must understand and support the project. If the congregation respects the integrity of each committee member, an element of trust is automatically generated in the committee's work.

5. Common sense: This is one that probably goes without saying, but things that go without saying are usually the things that should be said more often. Judgment can sometimes be clouded by insecurities or preconceived ideas. You want each member of the building committee to be able to evaluate each step along the way on its own merits and then make a decision that makes the most sense.

6. Independent team player: It is important for every building committee member to be free to express perceptions and opinions. If every member of the committee is able to do this, then the process builds on itself, resulting in quality ideas and direction that would not have been possible by any one person. At the same time, each member must be a team player so that when a decision is made, full support is given. You want all members of the committee to be independent enough to express their opinions and then support all decisions as though they were their own ideas. The first five qualifications make this a real possibility.

7. Varied background: Varied backgrounds of committee members will give you broader support from the congregation. It will also make it easier to incorporate opinions and ideas from a greater cross-section of the congregation. This is part of the genius of Abraham Lincoln during the Civil War years. His Cabinet was made up of people from all political backgrounds, including an opponent who followed Lincoln to heckle him during his campaign speeches.

8. Diligent worker: Most potential building committee members have a number of significant roles and responsibilities with the church, their families, their profession and their other interests. To be asked to be part of the building committee means a significant commitment of time and effort. Each member needs to be diligent enough to faithfully fulfill responsibilities on the committee without sacrificing other important areas of life.

9. Planning skills: It will be important to have people who have skills in analysis and decision-making. You also want to have a certain amount of creativity from people who are capable of thinking outside the box.

10. Knowledge of the building industry: Of the top 10 qualifications, this is the least important. You will be hiring the industry professionals necessary to help you physically design and build the facilities. What those industry professionals cannot do is tell you what your ministry should be. They can assist you in developing facilities to meet the ministry needs as expressed by the building committee. Knowledge of the building industry can be helpful, but it is no substitute for any of the other nine qualifications.

Absent from this list of qualifications is someone's status as a major financial contributor. This status shouldn't qualify or disqualify someone from serving on the building committee. Major contributors are an important part to many building programs. God has done some amazing things through the gifts and financial blessing of individuals. What must be avoided is the sense that a major contributor has more say in the building program than any other committee member has. No committee member should have more influence than another should. It is often through the freedom of expression from individuals with varied backgrounds and perspectives that the facilities with the greatest fit are developed. Major contributors are an important part of the process but make good building committee members only when they have the other 10 qualifications.

I worked with one church for five years before we were able to move ahead with the construction. There were a lot of internal challenges to deal with. This was evidenced by the fact that there were three different building committees throughout that five-year process. The chairman of the second building committee had not been at church for two years because of a dispute with another member. He was asked to come back to chair the committee only because his mother was the major contributor to the program. For obvious reasons, it wasn't until the third building committee was formed that we were able to make this project a reality.

The goal of the committee is certainly not for everyone to have the same approach or the same insights. But with the right attitudes, the committee can come together in support of what it believes is the best overall direction for the church given the strategic ministry plan. It is that sense of community that will help to ensure the right project. In an interview from Christianity Today, Rev. Bill Hybels of Willow Creek Community Church described it this way,

"At Willow Creek we expect disagreement – forceful disagreement. Unity isn't a word that we use to describe our relationships. Popular concept of unity is a fantasyland where disagreements never surface and contrary opinions are never stated with a force. Instead of unity, we use the word community. We say, 'Let's pretend that we never disagree.' We are dealing with the lives of 20,000 people where stakes are high. Let's not have people hiding their concerns to protect a false notion of unity. Let's face the disagreement and deal with it in a godly way. The mark of community – true Biblical unity – is not the absence of conflict; it's the presence of a reconciling spirit. I can have a rough and tumble meeting with somebody, but because we are committed to community, we can still leave slapping each other on the back, saying, 'I'm glad we are brothers.' We know no one is bailing out just because of a conflict in position."

LEADERSHIP AND THE CHAIRPERSON

Leadership is a major issue facing the church in general today. It is arguably the major challenge we face. Many of the problems the church has encountered can be traced to poor leadership. There is a tendency to manage affairs as we have always done. The answer to the question, "Who should serve?" is critical, but the answer to "Who should lead?" is even more so. While tradition has its place, so does the kind of new, bold steps that can be taken only by selfless leaders who can envision what can be and can impart that hope to those around them to make the vision a reality.

A building program craves a leader who is conscious of the past, objectively aware of the present and able to see what the mission of the church means for the future. You are asking the leader, the chairperson, to blend the talents, abilities and perspectives of the committee into a comprehensive, unified solution that is supported emotionally, intellectually and financially by the congregation. A building program deserves leadership commensurate with the task.

Leadership is a topic that has drawn a great deal of attention over the years. Tremendous resources are available from writers like Peter Drucker, John Maxwell, Warren Bennis, Ken Blanchard and others who provide invaluable insights into leadership in a way that makes it practically applicable. Here are a few insights as they apply to the chairperson.

The chairperson, like all the committee members, must exhibit the top 10 qualifications for building committee members. The chairperson should demonstrate the first three in abundance. The first two qualifications may be non-negotiable with the other committee members, but for the chairperson, the first three are non-negotiable.

An exemplary Christian life dictates a character of integrity. Integrity is a better word than truthful because integrity means wholeness – it means that, not only are the words truthful, but the person's thoughts, actions and intentions are all congruent with one another. John Maxwell says this is critical. "The first thing to look for in any kind of leader or potential leader is strength of character. I have found nothing more important than this quality. Serious character flaws cannot be ignored. They will eventually make a leader ineffective – every time."[1]

Integrity of character engenders trust. Trust is the common bond that binds the committee members together toward the common purpose. Maxwell said, "I have learned that trust is the single most important factor in building personal and professional relationships. Trust implies accountability, predictability and reliability. It calls for consistency."[1] Trust cannot be manipulated. Warren Bennis says, "Most of trust comes not from a particular technique, but from the character of the leader."[2] A leader with integrity is transparent, and no one needs to second-guess his motives.

An exemplary Christian life enables individuals to have a healthy self-image, handle stress, face problems without fear and take responsibility for their situations. They have a positive, confident attitude that is not encumbered by other people's perceptions. In "The Heart of a Leader," Ken Blanchard commented, "Observing successful leaders over the years, I have noticed that they don't let disappointments stop them. When one door closes, they look for another door to open."[3]

Being a life-long learner is a characteristic of all great leaders. A great leader does not assume he has the answers to all the questions but is willing to search for those answers and others throughout his life. Consider what Moses had to say toward the end of his life, as the Israelites were about to enter the Promised Land. "O sovereign Lord, you have begun to show your servant your greatness and your strong hand. For what God is there in heaven or on earth who can do the deeds and mighty works you do?" (NIV) Notice that even near the end of his life, Moses was still learning.

The second non-negotiable trait is a thorough understanding and uncompromising support of the strategic ministry objectives of the church. This is critical because you are not asking the chairperson to manage a static process. You are asking him to lead in the development of facilities that will significantly shape the ministry for the future. Therefore, the leader must clearly understand the mission of the church – where it is headed.

John P. Kotter, in his article, "What Leaders Really Do", recognizes that "leadership and management are two distinctive and complementary systems of action. Each has its own function and characteristic activities. Both are necessary for success."[4] Leadership is about effectiveness and asks the questions what and why, while management is about efficiency and asks the question how. Kotter goes on to explain that management brings "order and consistency," while leadership "is about coping with change."

Leadership is the ability to mobilize people synergistically to accomplish a goal. A leader must be able to inspire and empower people toward a vision that does not yet exist and then work with them to flesh out the steps to get there. A leader must be able to see the big picture, not be distracted by the crisis of the moment, and be able to work with abstract issues such as momentum and fatigue to facilitate the optimal performance of the committee. According to leadership expert Warren Bennis, "Leaders conquer the context – the turbulent, ambiguous surroundings that sometimes seem to conspire against us and will surely suffocate us if we let them."[5]

You are asking the chairperson to blaze a trail knowing only where you have come from, where you are and where you are headed. If the leader does not fully understand the mission of the church, there is not much chance the facilities will be well suited for that ministry.

The third non-negotiable factor is emotional intelligence. Emotional intelligence is the key to bringing synergy to the process. Synergy is simply making a group of people more effective than the sum of its parts. The person who is able to understand and marshal his emotions and who can understand what others are feeling has the greatest opportunity to influence those around him. That person is able to guide the relationships in a way that brings out the best of everybody.

One of the key skills of an emotionally intelligent leader is listening. Ken Blanchard said, "When you ask people about the best leader they ever had, the one quality that is always mentioned – they were good listeners."[6] Yet listening is not a skill that is born to some and deprived to others. According to Peter Drucker, "Listening is not a skill; it is a discipline. Anybody can do it."[7]

There is a fourth, previously unmentioned quality that is consistent with many of the great leaders I have known or studied. That quality is a paradoxical blend of humility and will. Jim Collins in his book *Good to Great* describes this as a level V leader. He said that:

"Level V Leaders are a study in duality: modest and willful, shy and fearless. To grasp this concept, consider Abraham Lincoln, who never let his ego get in the way of his ambition to create an enduring great nation. Author Henry Adams called him a quiet, peaceful, shy figure. But those who thought Lincoln's understated manner signaled weakness in the man found themselves terribly mistaken – to the scale of 250,000 Confederate and 360,000 Union lives, including Lincoln's own."

A leader is steely and focused, but a great leader combines that resolve with an attitude that lifts others above himself. Drucker said, "The leaders that work most effectively, it seems to me, never say I. And that is not because they have trained themselves not to say I. They don't think I. They think we; they think team."[8] Jesus is our greatest example in this combination of determined will and humility (Acts 2:5-11). Andrew Murray in his work titled, "Humility" asks us to examine the life of Christ and to "listen to his teaching. There we will hear how he speaks of it and how far he expects men, and especially his disciples, to be as humble as he was."

I became a good friend with a number of committee members who I had the opportunity to work with. One chairman called to tell me about an experience he had while researching the history of past building programs. He noted that in all of his research, he never found the names of the people who had served on prior building committees. It reinforced to him that he is not there to serve for the recognition of man. He is there to serve the Lord. I think he got it.

The building committee chairperson may not be the most prominent or most likely selection on the surface. If you look at the way God has selected leaders throughout the Bible, you notice that he often selects the least likely to lead in the most difficult task. Seeking God's heart in this matter will help you identify the right leader.

Remember that identifying a leader and giving him or her the title does not make the leader. Leadership can only come from what is inside the individual. Leadership comes from inside. Look at who is willing to follow them now. Determine if they are capable of bringing about change. A leader will have demonstrated the ability to exert influence to make things happen.

I found the quality of the chairperson's work to be gender neutral. In fact, women chaired two of the most well executed committees I had the opportunity to serve. They commanded the respect of the committee and diligently worked to accomplish what was best for the church without preconceived ideas or agendas.

The role of the pastor and staff varies dramatically from one church to another. Some churches believe that the pastor is there to lead the church and it is his or her vision for the church that must be pursued through the strategic ministry plan and resulting facilities. At the other end of the spectrum, some churches view the pastor as someone they have simply hired for a certain period of time to assist the membership in the ministry of the church. Most churches find themselves somewhere within that spectrum.

Wherever you are on that spectrum, it is important to think through this role so that you can blend the insights, skills, passions and desires of the pastor and staff with those of the membership. As I read the scriptures, there is no longer a separation between clergy and laity; we are all called to be priests. Those we refer to as the clergy are really the full-time paid staff who are there to equip the body of Christ to do the work of the ministry. You will want to think through these roles as they relate to the leadership of the church and your building program.

ORGANIZATION

Since there is seemingly an infinite number of ways to structure committees to accomplish a building program, the first activity is to decide on the structure. You may have one building committee that handles all of the processes or you could conceivably have as many as 15-20 committees/subcommittees. In general, the larger the church the more committees/ subcommittees you are likely to have. One reason for this is that, in larger churches, more legwork is required of the committee. Another reason is that there is greater potential for competencies in a wider range of areas of expertise.

Having more people involved through committees and subcommittees is normally a good idea. People who are involved in the process tend to have more ownership in the project, which means they are likely to champion the project in their sphere of influence in the congregation and will also be more engaged in giving to the project. However, there is also a down side to having a great number of people involved in the process. I worked with a church that decided to select two color schemes and then leave it open to the congregation for a vote. Initially that seemed like a good idea, but what you end up with is a far greater number of people who are dissatisfied with whatever color is selected than would be if the building committee had just selected the colors. You must be able to manage effectively whatever depth of committee structure you deem appropriate.

There are two primary reasons for expanding the committee structure. There may be specific areas of expertise within the congregation that you want to bring to bear on the project. Those individuals may not be the right people for the building committee, but they have a talent (i.e., financial planning, landscaping, education and daycare) that would be helpful. You may also have an area that needs special attention. For instance, you may be considering relocation. In that case, a subcommittee of the building committee could be formed for that purpose.

The number of subcommittees you have will be limited by the amount of meaningful tasks that can be delegated by the depth of leadership and management skills on the building committee. The building committee must serve as the executive committee with all other committees and subcommittees reporting to and through it. The building committee has the big-picture perspective to be able to evaluate alternatives and make decisions as well as provide direction.

There are three keys to making a structure work once it has been set up:
1. Responsibility
2. Authority
3. Communication

It is critical that as the leadership establishes the building committee it must be crystal clear on what the committee is to accomplish. Then it must endow the committee with authority commensurate with the responsibilities. The link between the leadership and the building committee and between the building committee and any other subcommittee needs to be active two-way communication. It is not good enough to be able to say, "We told them." You have to know there is a clear understanding of what needs to be done and where you are throughout the process.

The committee needs to be seen as representative of and responsive to the congregation. It has to be sensitive to what the congregation is feeling and, at the appropriate times and in the appropriate ways, solicit input from the congregation. This will not only improve the overall project but will also expand the sense of ownership to many more members of the congregation.

FINANCE COMMITTEE

The most significant potential subcommittee is the finance committee. A single common characteristic of the hundreds of church projects we have served is that every one of them had adequate funding. The role of projecting the funds that will be available and then procuring those funds falls to this committee.

The simplest structure is when the building committee also serves as the finance committee (see Exhibit 4A). The obvious advantage to this approach is the coordination and communication between the financial and spatial scopes of the project. However, this puts a tremendous workload on one committee. To make this model work, the building committee would either have to oversimplify some important tasks or make good use of the legwork that can be provided through subcommittees.

Exhibit 4A

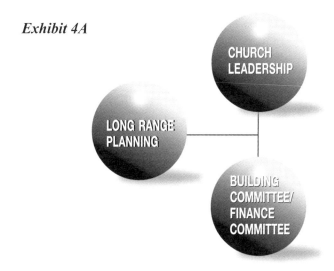

A similar approach would be where the leadership maintains the control of the finance committee. This can be a simple model as well, with the leadership providing the financial parameters to the building committee along with its charge to develop the facilities. The potential advantage here is that the leadership will have intimate awareness of the projected financial picture. But this would be placing a lot of work into the hands of the leadership that also has responsibility for leading and managing the affairs of the church.

A third possible model would be separate building and finance committees that are established by the leadership (see Exhibit 4B). This has the advantage of putting these two monumental tasks into two competent committees. This may also be an option to a church that has a standing finance committee that is already dealing with the long-range and day-to-day financial aspects of the church. The charge of the financing for the building project could be added to its plate.

Exhibit 4B

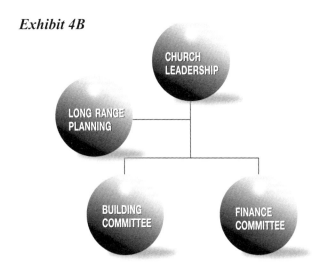

For this to work, extra steps would have to be taken to ensure the coordination between the building committee and the finance committee. Since they were set up as independent committees, they can sometimes see their role as so distinct that they head in different directions. There have been a lot of churches that have run into problems with a presumptuous attitude that says, "We'll just design what we think we need and let the finance committee worry about how to pay for it."

A model of that deals well with the communication and coordination between the building committee and finance committee as one where the finance committee serves as a subcommittee to the building committee (see Exhibit 4C). Presumably, as a subcommittee, the work of the finance committee is likely to be more closely matched with the efforts of the building committee. With the importance of this subcommittee, it should not just report to and take direction from the building committee. There should be more overlap of committee members. Ideally, at least the chairman of the finance committee should be a member of the building committee.

Exhibit 4C

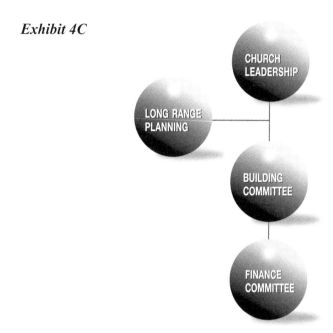

OTHER COMMITTEES/SUBCOMMITTEES

There are an abundance of other possible committees or subcommittees that you might consider for your building program. The number of committees will depend on what facets are particularly important to your ministry and what expertise you have in the congregation. It is good to involve many people, but it is important to keep it to a manageable number.

The appropriate number of subcommittees for your church will be a balance between the leadership capabilities of the building committee and involving as much of the time and talents of the congregation as possible. Identify the important aspects of the project that could be enhanced through the detailed work of a subcommittee. Secondly, look to the congregation for what unique capabilities exist. Finally, look at the leadership capabilities of the building committee to be sure that all of these areas can be properly managed to make a positive impact.

Below you will find possible ideas on committees. You may think of many more as you read through this section. The arrangement you choose may be significantly different than what is shown. The committee structure should work for you to meet your needs.

One possible subcommittee could deal with the property. If you are considering relocation or an additional campus for your ministry, then you may wish to have a property study/selection committee to assist in identifying and advising on new locations. There are many issues such as zoning and wetlands than can dramatically affect the desirability and function of a site. Input from a site design committee might be helpful while the design of the buildings is taking place. It could advise the main committee, perhaps through subcommittees, on landscaping, signage and site lighting.

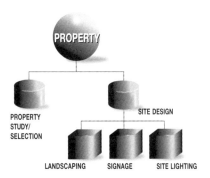

Some of the obvious and more common subcommittees deal with the function of the facilities. One such committee could be a worship center committee. There may be subcommittees dealing with sound and video, furnishings, seating and windows.

Another facility committee could deal with Christian education. Some of the normal subcommittees to Christian education would include daycare, nursery, preschool, elementary, high school and adult. Any one of these can be broken down further into sub-subcommittees as necessary. For instance, adult Christian education may have separate subcommittees dealing with singles, couples or senior adults.

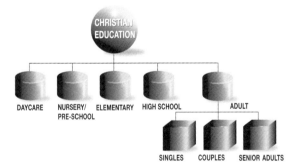

Fellowship is another common subcommittee, particularly when the new facilities are likely to contain a family life center or fellowship hall. The fellowship committee may have two subcommittees: food and activities. The food committee could be broken down further into banquets and dinners, and the activities committee could be divided between general recreation and sports.

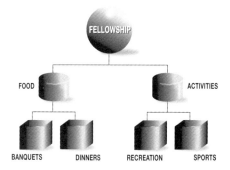

Administration is an area that often does not have a committee. This is probably because it is generally felt that the staff has access to or is part of the building committee. If this is not the case, then an administration committee could assist in the development of the facilities that would serve the staff. You may also have a large volunteer staff participating on a day-to-day basis in the ministry of the church. An administrative committee could help in discovering what kind of space would serve those volunteers best.

The areas of ministries and missions are two that could have numerous uses in the form of committees or subcommittees. The ministries committee could have subcommittees dealing with small groups, special programs, evangelism and discipleship. The missions committee could be divided into local mission and foreign missions.

LOCAL MISSIONS · FOREIGN MISSIONS · OTHER MISSIONS

Another committee or subcommittee that is often overlooked is promotion/publicity. Both before and during the building program there are opportunities to get positive press on the church. This committee could serve to make sure that positive press happens in a coordinated way to have the maximum impact through exposure impact. It would also be helpful in any capital stewardship campaign you may be considering. A promotional/publicity committee would deal with the internal and external audiences.

Whether there is a separate legal committee or you get specific legal counsel directly to the building committee, it is important to make this a part of the process. Legal counsel can help you to be thoroughly informed about what you are signing. Legal counsel also may be necessary for re-zoning, permit and variance issues in some parts of the country. Any legal counsel sought in this process should be experienced in issues related to church projects.

A committee that is sometimes activated toward the end of the design phase and the beginning of the construction phase is the construction committee. This committee might review the construction documents for questions or possible discrepancies. It also could administer the construction throughout the construction phase by advising on contract change orders and other adjustments. For this subcommittee to be successful, it must thoroughly understand the discussions and decisions that led to the design.

The final subcommittee is one that, unfortunately, is rarely seen. The role of the assimilation committee would be to help the church maximize the impact of the new facility as it moves from the way things used to be to how things can be with the new facilities. The committee could organize prayer groups, help with publicity and perform other duties to help with the transition. It is important to remember that the completion of a building program is not the end of the race but rather a means to run stronger and faster and do more.

The intention here is not to imply that you must have a lot of committees/subcommittees but rather to spark ideas so that you can match the right structure to the leadership and management abilities of the building committee. Then you can take full advantage of the competencies available in the church and address the key issues that will be part of your building program. The right mix is as unique as every church. Just remember to balance the number of subcommittees with meaningful work and adequate leadership.

PLAN THE COMMITTEE ACTIVITIES

The first step of the building committee is to actively seek to understand what is to be accomplished after the completion of the building program. What are the ministry needs that are to be addressed through the addition and renovation of facilities? Without this understanding, the likelihood of a successful building program is a shot in the dark. A beautiful, affordable building can be a waste of time and money if it does not appropriately and adequately meet the ministry needs.

The second step is to actively seek to understand the financial parameters related to the project. Depending on the committee structure and the role of the church leadership, this may simply be an awareness of the project budget limits. In most cases, however, the responsibility for establishing the project budget considerations falls to the building (finance) committee. This must be a proactive step that generates financial parameters the committee is committed to work within throughout the project.

Armed with a thorough understanding of the purpose for the building program and a keen awareness of the financial picture, the building committee can continue to move forward to identify and engage the industry professionals. The building committee will decide on the project delivery method that best suits its needs, then select the industry professionals that provide the greatest character and competence. The committee will work with the industry professionals to master plan and then design the needed facilities. The final step before construction will be to secure the funds to complete the project.

Another one of those activities involves congregational and/or church approvals. If you are part of a denomination, you will want to research when approvals are required and by whom. There may be certain notification qualifications that must be followed by your denominational disciplines. If you are not part of a denomination, you will want, at the very least, to get approval from the congregation. Even if this is not technically required by your church policy, it can be instrumental in securing their support of and contribution toward the building program.

COMMUNICATION

Communication is another essential responsibility of the building committee. Through the timely dissemination of information, the building committee can build understanding, awareness and support for the project that can help to maximize the impact of the new facility. There are three primary entities with which the building committee can communicate: church leadership, congregation and community.

Dialogue with the church leadership about the key building committee decisions and directions will help to make sure the project stays on track. This communication is particularly pertinent in the early phases. It allows the church leadership to be aware of the progress and gives the building committee a means to request any clarification of priorities or purpose.

Communication with the congregation will likely be less detailed and less frequent than with the church leadership. It is critical to have the congregation on board in any building project to ensure its support emotionally, financially and prayerfully. This can be an ongoing process but is more necessary during the early phases of the project when there is nothing tangible for the congregation to see.

Finally, communication to the community can be an opportunity for the church. A building program can raise interest in and awareness of the ministries of the church. The building committee should be conscious of how to get the information to the community.

Two means for communicating with the community involve advertising and publicity. Either form works best when it is built around an event, such as a groundbreaking service, erection of the steeple or completion of the project. Many local print and broadcast media would be willing to cover those events because they are newsworthy for the community.

Churches that are the most successful in publicizing their new or expanded facility usually form a publicity team early in the process. The team (or possible subcommittee) would be responsible for identifying the broadcast and print media opportunities. It would be responsible for identifying the newsworthy events and guiding the communication through press releases and photography.

[1] John Maxwell. Developing the Leaders Around You. Nashville, TN. Thomas Nelson, Inc. 1995
[2] Warren Bennis, Joan Goldsmith. Learning to Lead. Reading, MA. Addison-Wesley Publishing. 1997
[3] Ken Blanchard. The Heart of a Leader. Tulsa, OK. Honor Books. 1999
[4] John P. Kotter. Harvard Business Review. May/June 1990
[5] Bennis, Goldsmith. Learning to Lead
[6] Blanchard The Heart of the Leader.
[7] Peter Drucker. Managing the Non-Profit Organization
[8] Drucker. Managing the Non-Profit Organization

Before You Build
Chapter 5- Before You Budget

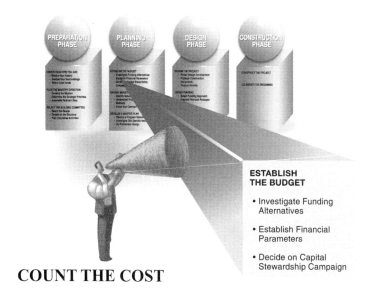

**ESTABLISH
THE BUDGET**

• Investigate Funding
  Alternatives

• Establish Financial
  Parameters

• Decide on Capital
  Stewardship Campaign

COUNT THE COST

I have been involved in hundreds of building programs over the past couple of decades. Some of those were small, simple places of worship, and others were large auditoriums with stadium seating. Some included additional educational space, and others were full-fledged Christian schools. Some were fellowship halls to serve simple meals Wednesday night, and others were family life centers that could accommodate banquets, basketball games, volleyball matches, bowling, racquetball and physical conditioning. Some were extremely intricate and ornate and, consequently very expensive. Others were very plain and direct. But all of these projects had one thing in common: the dollars to complete them.

Throughout the years, there have been congregations that were able to pay cash, and others borrowed what was needed through a variety of lending options. In most cases, it was a combination of the two. Often it included a capital stewardship campaign that may have been directed by a company that specializes in capital campaigns. Some churches attempted their own campaigns.

When adequate funding is not there, the result can be disastrous. I remember reading of a church in Fort Myers, Fla., which had taken on a project serving as its own general contractor. With the building partially completed and the funds gone, the church went bankrupt and lost its property. From all I could learn about this project, it appeared the leadership did not adequately count the cost.

Jesus speaks to this, in a sense, in Luke 14:25. By this time in Christ's ministry, the crowds were getting very large because people had begun to follow Jesus for many reasons. Some followed him out of curiosity or to see the miracles they'd heard about. Others followed out of the compassion they saw in his eyes or the tenderness of his spirit. He turned to address them on what it meant to be a true follower of Jesus Christ and admonished them to count the cost of becoming a disciple.

One of the analogies Jesus uses is found in verses 28-30. He asked the people who would begin to build a tower without first determining the cost and whether they had enough money to complete it. To not finish it would subject them to ridicule. The thrust of this scripture is to show that we are to count the cost of becoming a disciple of Jesus Christ. However, using this analogy, Jesus makes it clear that it is wise to count the cost of what you are going to build and to make sure you have the funds before you begin.

Most projects that are over-designed or run short of funds do not end up with the devastation the church in Fort Myers experienced. Instead, many are scaled back late in the process by eliminating important square footage or needed furnishings and equipment. Sometimes it means the elimination of staff or specific ministries to pay for the building. These cutbacks may not be as visible as a church that loses its property, but the results can be consequential nonetheless.

The greatest tragedy is that in nearly every case these situations are avoidable. It is simply a matter of understanding what dollars are available and then working with the industry professionals to design and build a facility that meets your ministry needs and that stays within budget. Be aware of a few safeguards to help you to stay on track.

BE REALISTIC

Some programs get off on the wrong foot because a driving force on the building committee has an unrealistic expectation of what the building process will cost. Perhaps he remembers the numbers from the last building program and wants to draw comparisons. However, what may not be evident is the increase in inflation. Or the building completed in the past could be an entirely different style than the current building, leading to an overly optimistic or overly pessimistic view of what the new building might cost. I have seen assumptions of church building costs based on a home, warehouse or some other commercial or industrial building. And some of those buildings were several years old. In nearly all of those cases the numbers were inapplicable and misleading.

The concept of comparisons is valid, but what makes it applicable is having more meaningful comparisons to give you the most accurate range of building costs that you are likely to encounter. What is also important is that you establish the range from a multitude of examples and information. This information will not tell you what your specific facility will cost, but it will educate you to a likely base range. Then your industry professional should be able to explain what specifically needs to be done in the design to be at the upper or lower end of that range and what factors will pull it out of that range.

For example, say you knew nothing about the new car market in the United States, but you wanted to know what a new car might cost. You could imagine how misleading it would be if you based your perception on what your neighbor down the street had paid for his new car. Your perception would vary dramatically depending on whether he bought a compact economy sedan or a $250,000 Lamborghini.

Several sources can help with establishing the range of potential costs for a building. R.S. Means is a national company that tracks cost data related to specific building types. McGraw Hill, Dodge Reports and Construction Market Data are other companies that compile information. Getting cost information from recently completed projects in your area also can be useful.

Comparing square-footage costs (the overall cost divided by the number of square feet in the building) is a common approach to gaining valuable information. Divide the cost of the building by its square footage to get a per square foot rate. It is a common method for comparing the relative cost of facilities that may be dramatically different in size. It can be useful as a general guide if you understand the variables that affect square-footage costs, but here is a strong word of caution: It cannot tell you exactly what the cost of your facility will be.

Lack of a full understanding of the pitfalls of square-footage pricing can be very misleading and do more harm than good. The numerator for calculating cost per square foot is the building cost. It is extremely important to understand what is and is not included in the building cost. Does the estimate include architectural fees? What about site-preparation costs? Don't forget about furnishings.

The denominator in the calculation is the square footage. If the calculation of the square footage is off, the cost per square foot will obviously be incorrect. I was working with a church in

Tampa that commented about the cost per square foot of another church in that city. I was aware of the project, and the cost per square foot seemed low for that building. The church was gracious enough to give us a copy of the last invoice so we knew what exactly had been paid to the contractor. It also provided us with a set of the construction drawings so we could calculate the square footage. What we found was that the actual cost per square foot was 50 percent higher than what had been reported because it was based on a factor that did not make it into the final project.

Over and over again I hear the question, "What does a church cost per square foot?" One of the best answers is an analogy that asks another question. "What does a bag of groceries cost?" Obviously, the cost of a bag of groceries is determined by what goes in it. It is the same way with church facilities – the cost per square foot is determined by what goes into the building.

A major impact to cost per square foot is the structure itself. By structure I simply mean the system for supporting the walls and roof. A simple structure might have block walls and flat bottom cord wood trusses on a 4/12 pitch. A more expensive solution would be laminated arches and wood deck on a 10/12 pitch. Depending on the spans and complexity of the building, steel can be less expensive, particularly in larger facilities. The complexity of the structure will affect costs. In general, the more complex, the more gables, the more windows, or the more corners added to a building, the higher the cost.

The level of finish is another factor that affects cost per square foot. It is easy to see how a building with a painted block exterior would be less expensive than a block wall faced with brick. The same principle applies for the interior. An interior wall finished with drywall is obviously going to be more expensive than simply painting the block. Crown molding, chair rails and relief paneling add beauty and warmth but also cost. Ceramic tile on the floor of restrooms is more expensive than vinyl tile but less expensive than running that ceramic tile to Wainscot height or all the way up the walls. Various types of carpet, light figures, doors and hardware are finish factors that influence the quality and cost of a building.

The building's primary systems (heating, ventilation, air conditioning, electrical and plumbing) can drive the square-footage costs in different directions. Sound and computer systems also add to the price. The restrooms are typically expensive square footage, so the relative number, size and location of the restrooms are factors that will vary the cost. Trying to cut costs with the primary systems can create problems later. For instance, a less-sophisticated heating and air conditioning system may save money, but if it's so noisy that it prevents people from hearing a message in the sanctuary, then more money will be spent to correct that problem.

Local building codes also can affect costs. Most coastal areas require a building to withstand certain wind loads. Just a few miles further inland, the wind load requirements may be less, which would reduce the cost. Safety and fire code interpretations can also have a dramatic impact costs. One of the greatest areas of variation from one area to the next is in the site development requirements including drainage, water retention, landscaping, parking and paving, site lighting, finish floor elevations, buffers and sidewalks.

One thing that will affect cost per square foot is the relative size of one facility to another. All things being equal, a 21,000-square-foot facility will cost less per square foot than a comparable facility at 14,000 square feet. Part of the reason for this is that while the project is 50 percent larger, it will not likely take 50 percent longer to build, so there are savings in general conditions and overhead. And the larger facility will generally not require 50 percent more in some of the high cost areas such as restrooms. This doesn't always hold true, given the larger structure may get into other complexity issues such as structural spans. But it is a good rule of thumb.

One thing that will definitely impact the cost per square foot is the cubic footage. A 10,000-square-foot sanctuary with 20-foot high walls is going to be more expensive than a comparably designed sanctuary with 12-foot walls. Not only are there additional materials in the additional 8 feet of the walls, including block, brick, wood, drywall and paint, but there are also increased areas that must be heated and cooled, plus the costs of lighting, acoustics and other accessories.

In developing church facilities, the cost of a two-by-four or block or cubic yard of concrete will not vary much from contractor to contractor. The labor rates and quality will vary a little more, and the way the contractor supervises the construction and manages the business and overhead will vary even more. But, no one has the capability to build a comparable quality facility for half or even three-quarters of anyone else.

BUDGETING

Budgeting is a key step that is often overlooked in building programs. By budgeting, I am referring to the preliminary analysis of the church's financial situation to begin to establish a possible project budget. At first, it is based on assumptions and rules of thumb that should continue to be refined throughout the development process. A possible project budget is established not to be able to spend everything that is available but rather to provide an awareness of the limits and a means by which you can prioritize the allocation of your resources. Many building projects will push the financial limits of the church, so it is necessary to know where those limits are.

One of the simplest rules of thumb to get you into the ballpark is the equation: three times annual income plus cash minus debt. Begin by looking at the actual income raised for all purposes last year regardless of what was budgeted. If the trend of the annual income is up over prior years, multiply that amount by three and add to it any cash that is available to be funneled into the building program. From that amount subtract any outstanding debt the church has, and you will arrive at a preliminary project budget number.

For example, if a church has $500,000 in annual income, $325,000 cash on hand and $75,000 in debt, the calculation would work as follows:

Annual Income	$500,000
	X3
	$1,500,000
Cash on Hand	$325,000
Subtotal	$1,825,000
Debt	-$75,000
Possible Project Budget	$1,750,000

Having property to sell can increase the cash portion of the budget equation. What is important here is to make sure the property can be sold in the time frame necessary to positively affect the project budget. In most cases, it will take longer than you think. In fact, if you are considering a relocation project that requires the sale of property, it will normally extend the life of the building program at least one year. And that is often the time it takes for the church leaders to work through the painful awareness that their property is not worth what they thought it might be.

You might also have a greater debt service capacity if you have debt service monies in your budget and the payoff of the debt is relatively low. Say you were paying $10,000 a month on a debt that had $100,000 left. That current monthly amount could be enough (depending on interest rates and the term of the loan) to amortize $1,000,000, which would enable you to borrow a net of $900,000 through your current budget.

The bottom line is that the dollars need to be there to be able to complete the project. If financing is involved, then the dollars need to be there to be able to pay the debt. These rules of thumb will move you toward the right range, but further refinement of the budget will need to take place throughout the project, specifically identifying where debt service dollars will come from.

The calculation of income above should not include money from schools or day cares. However, if there is residual income from the operation of these ministries, it will add to the payback capability of the church. Likewise, if there is a yearly deficit, it will reduce dollars available for debt service. These are more complicated calculations that your industry professionals should be able to assist you in understanding and in how they will affect your project.

A word of caution: This is a project budget number, not a building budget number. Most of the time when churches are investigating or discussing the cost of the facility, they are referring to the building cost only. There are many costs that make up the project cost. Please see Exhibit 5-A for an example of a sample project budget. This sample includes just some of the potential items you may encounter in your building program.

You will notice that one of the line items at the end of the sample project budget in Exhibit 5-A is contingency. This is a valuable line item to keep as part of the project budget from the planning phase through the construction phase. As the major cost components of the project are known, the amount you carry in contingency can be reduced. Building and site costs are usually the two largest components that make up the overall project costs. Once these and any other major components unique to your project are known, the contingency can be reduced. In general, it might be wise to use 25 percent to 30 percent for contingency in the early planning stages and refine that down to about 5 percent during construction.

Keep in mind that there is always the potential for surprises. For instance, you may have a firm price on your building and site costs and you find out during excavation that there is an old fuel tank in the ground that went undetected by soil borings. The cost of removing that tank would be the property owner's responsibility. The same may be true for other issues such as code interpretations. Even the project delivery method you select and the specific industry professionals you choose may influence the amount of contingency you carry. Design disputes that arise during the construction phase with the design/bid/build delivery method will likely result in additional costs to the owner, but in the design/build method, they are usually the responsibility of the design builder. Even if the contingency is not needed for surprises, it may be beneficial to have to take advantage of opportunities that are recognized during construction that no one thought of before you got to that point.

The church budget for future years will obviously need to incorporate the monthly payments needed to amortize any indebtedness incurred by the building project. There will be other costs related to the building that will also have an impact on future church budgets. There will obviously be additional utility costs with the new square footage, increased janitorial and maintenance costs, and additional staff costs to fully administrate the new facilities.

INVESTIGATE FUNDING ALTERNATIVES

Investigating the potential funding sources that are available to you is a good way to develop insights into what you may be able to afford. Begin your dialogues early with banks, bond companies and other potential viable sources (see Chapter 8). You can begin to gauge subjective factors like their level of interest and secure objective information such as limits on funding and a percentage of pledges they will consider for debt service. Most banks, credit unions and bond companies, especially those that specialize in lending to churches, will give you an idea of a project budget per your current financial information.

Get as much specific information as possible in writing along with a letter of interest or commitment. I have seen a number of churches be unintentionally misled from a broad preliminary discussion from a lender. The pastor may indicate to a lender they have done business with for years that they are planning a building program and will be borrowing funds. That lender indicates that he is very interested in lending the money to the church, and the church takes from that conversation that it is able to borrow whatever it needs. What the lender meant was that he was interested in looking at the package to consider a loan. Do not be misled by kind words spoken in abstract.

The churches that are in the best position financially tend to be the ones that have planned. In some ways it is like planning for a child's college education. Saving early makes it much more productive down the road. It can sometimes be difficult to raise money for a project that it is not imminent. People are more apt to give to something they can see and touch. But stewardship is the key to the life of the church and should always be preached. Long-range financial planning should be a key component to long-range ministry planning.

DONATED LABOR AND MATERIALS

A church can sometimes have access to donated labor and materials. It is good to make use of these opportunities, but it is important to make sure they are, in fact, legitimate opportunities. We worked with one church that indicated it had a plumber (loosely affiliated with the church) that was willing to donate his labor and provide the fixtures at his cost for the church. However, when we evaluated his donated labor and the costs of his materials, he was more expensive than other plumbers.

Another way that donated labor can be a hindrance is if it gets less attention from the provider because it's free. If donated time extends the project deadline, it is very possible it may cost more in the long run. It is important that the individual or company providing the donated labor take on your project with every bit of energy and excellence they would with any other work. I have seen projects where masons took vacation time to lay the block on the project, making a tremendous positive contribution to the project. I have also seen lagging costs mount up because the project got attention only when the contractor had extra time.

There is much less donated labor on church projects today than there was years ago. This is largely because of stringent licensing requirements of many jurisdictions. Most municipalities require subcontractors to be tested and licensed to work in their area. Often key subcontractors must sign and give their license number before a permit can be issued on a project. The purpose is to increase quality and safety and eliminate unlicensed contractors. You will obviously not want to use unlicensed contractors in trades that are required by your area to be licensed. Likewise, it is every bit as unethical and illegal for an unlicensed subcontractor to borrow someone else's license number, even if he is donating his time. All labor, donated or not, must conform to all safety standards for OSHA, workers compensation and other applicable regulations.

Donated materials should also not drive the project. If someone is able to donate a certain type of concrete block, that donation should be considered. However, if the design has to be altered to the detriment of the facility to incorporate the donated block, then the donation should be respectfully declined. The main thing to keep in mind with donated labor and materials is to not let them drive the budget. You want to be sure that these donations are everything they appear to be before you make adjustments to the project budget. Planning for donations that don't pan out leads to disappointment in the people who fell short but also devastation that the project cannot proceed as designed.

BUILDING FOR CASH

There is another rule of thumb that you will want to keep in mind throughout the budgeting process. Have no more than one-third of your annual income going for debt service. That should be the maximum. Anymore than that may severely hamper your ministry. In fact, the less the better. As a general rule, you should be working toward little or no debt.

When a church is committed to build for cash, it simplifies the project budget formula to this: cash on hand minus debt. With most churches, it is even simpler than that since they probably have had that commitment for some time, so there is no debt. The project budget then simply equals whatever cash is available. Some churches may go through a capital stewardship campaign raising cash and pledges over a three-year period. Some will then take out a short-term loan to be fully amortized by the time the pledges are in at the end of the three-year period.

I have worked with churches that vehemently defend their positions on either side of the cash vs. borrowing debate. Each church must decide which approach is best. If the building is truly the barrier to growth and a church cannot build what it needs without borrowing, is it short-changing the ministry by not reaching the people it could be if it borrowed? On the other hand, are churches that consistently build for cash able to do more in ministry because they are not strapped with debt service?

For some churches, it may be a stand against borrowing that they believe is Biblically based. If so, they need to hold to that belief. For the rest it is a question of how to maximize the ministry. Could some borrowing enable a church to get into a facility that could expand ministry, or would those funds be better spent in staff and ministry resources? The counsel I would offer is to seek the Lord, recognizing that building for cash may delay a project significantly vs. the risk of borrowing. Even if the project is delayed, it must outpace inflation on the cost of the facility.

If you believe in a biblical mandate to build for cash, you must remain true to that belief. But if you aspire to build debt-free because it is prudent, consider moving in that direction given the guidelines above.

CAPITAL STEWARDSHIP CAMPAIGNS

Whether you are building for cash or borrowing, stewardship is a key biblical principle. It is my understanding that Jesus had more to say about stewardship than any other subject. With the prominence that Jesus gave to stewardship, it should not be a principle that we shy away from.

The building program is an opportune time for a capital stewardship campaign. Most are designed around an approach that will ask for cash and commitments over a three-year period. Some churches take on this campaign on their own, believing that they know their people better than someone from the outside. It is possible, though, that familiarity could hamper a stewardship campaign.

There are some excellent companies that specialize in capital stewardship campaigns. They are prayer-based and are able to tap into the spiritual ramifications of giving. Revivals have taken place when members of a congregation recognize that we do not own what we think we have – we are only stewards for a period of time. As stewards, we need to know what God would have us do with those possessions.

There are costs and risks involved in hiring a company to handle your capital stewardship campaign. But from the figures I have seen and the experiences we have had, I can tell you that they are better at communicating the purpose of the program and tapping into the heart of a congregation so it experiences the joy of giving. And their numbers bear out their success. Programs directed by the church tend to generate only about one-fourth the amount typically raised by reputable companies. I would highly recommend enlisting the services of a reputable company to manage your capital stewardship campaign.

There are some important things to keep in mind in hiring a capital stewardship company. In the Appendix you will find a questionnaire that can be used during the interview process that will help you draw out the information you need to make an informed decision. One of the most important things to do is to meet the actual consultant who will be doing your program to be sure you have the right fit.

Exhibit 5-A

SAMPLE PROJECT BUDGET

Building cost and architectural fees	$1,000,000
Sound and video system	85,000
Acoustical treatment	20,000
Special lighting	25,000
Furnishings, fixtures and equipment	135,000
Removal of hazardous material in old connector	8,000
Demolition of old connector	12,000
Re-roofing of existing building at tie-in	23,000
Site work including:	298,000

    a. Tree removal
    b. Soil testing and borings
    c. Grading, fill and compaction of soil
    d. Detention pond and swales
    e. Retaining walls
    f. Utility connections
    g. Relocation of electrical transformer
    h. Sidewalks
    i. Landscaping
    j. Curb cut
    k. Acceleration/deceleration lanes
    l. Site lighting
    m. Paving

Tap, permit, impact fees	20,000
Builder's risk	5,000
Payment and performance bond	12,000
Legal fees	7,000
Contingency	100,000

TOTAL POTENTIAL PROJECT BUDGET   **$1,750,000**

Before You Build
Chapter 6- Before You Hire the Professionals

ENGAGE INDUSTRY PROFESSIONALS

- Identify Industry Professionals
- Understand Project Delivery Methods
- Know Your Contract

INDUSTRY PROFESSIONALS

Every successful church expansion project includes the services of key professionals. Sometimes these professionals are friends or members of the church. Other times they are selected from the community. Often they will come from outside the community because of their area of specialization. These professionals are individuals who have particular areas of knowledge and expertise that will partner with the church leadership to bring the project into existence.

One of the most important responsibilities of the building committee is the selection of these professionals. These partnerships form the team that will drive the success of the project. The industry professionals that are common to nearly every project include the architect, engineers (structural, plumbing, mechanical and electrical) and contractor. These are the industry professionals who typically come to mind when we think of a building program, and we will discuss the selection process of these professionals in more detail.

Professionals who deal with the development of the site play an increasing role in the development of church projects. Regulations regarding site development encompass myriad issues, some of which could severely limit the area of development or render some sites incapable of development. Wetlands that can contain certain species of plants and animals are excluded from development except in extreme circumstances. The discovery of ancient artifacts or an endangered species could eliminate an area of property from development for a period of time or forever.

There are also site issues that deal with zoning, setbacks, buffering and landscaping. There is a need to get utilities to the site and the building. The conditions of the soil must be confirmed or engineered to be able to adequately carry the building loads. Water detention and retention, green space, parking and site lighting must all be engineered to the requirements and specifications of the local jurisdictions.

Civil engineers are the primary industry professionals who will assist in the site services. They will design the site to address the issues mentioned above and be sure that the conditions meet or exceed the requirements of all applicable codes. Normally this will also require the services of a surveyor to measure and plot the property, existing facilities, utility locations and topography. Soil testing also must be done for an engineer to certify the conditions and how they will affect the specific structure. The architect and/or contractor will be able to assist you in the selection of these site services.

Many states and local municipalities have restrictions on where and when buildings of a certain use can be developed. Normally this is done through zoning ordinances, so it is a matter of checking to see what your property is zoned to be sure a church is a permitted use. If a church is a not permitted under your current zoning but you have had a church there for some time, a grandfather clause may apply, and you may be granted permission to continue to expand. In other areas, even though the church has been in existence for years, the municipality may require you to get a variance or special exception before it will allow an expansion.

There are some areas where a church is not a permitted use in any zoning classification, which requires every church to get a special exception before a building is permitted. Some states require conditional use permits or special use permits before they will allow a church to develop facilities. In some cases variances may be required to be able to exceed a height restriction, encroach on a setback requirement or adjust a parking ratio requirement. Often the architect and/or contractor along with the civil engineer can assist you in securing these permits. In other cases, it will require the services of an attorney to direct this process.

An attorney will also be necessary in other areas. If the purchase of property is necessary for your expansion, you will want the advice of a real estate attorney. You will also want an attorney's advice on contracts with other industry professionals.

The specific area of experience and expertise is important in the selection of any industry professional. The greater the potential impact (monetarily or administratively), the more important it is to have professionals with experience and expertise in the specific area of consideration. It is important to select industry professionals who can demonstrate a successful history in the services they will provide.

Most churches do not realize that the fees paid to all the industry professionals represent a relatively small percentage of the initial cost of the facility. Yet, they are the ones that will play the largest part in determining the functional capabilities and the vast majority of the cost of the project. When you add the life cycle costs of maintenance, repair and utilities, the percentage that you pay the industry professionals becomes minute.

PROJECT DELIVERY METHODS

The team members with whom the church will have the most significant relationship include the architect and the contractor. How the contracts structure the relationships between those two entities and the church depends on the project delivery method. The project delivery method is the approach and the organization of these three roles to design and build the needed facilities.

There are many categories to consider when discussing project delivery methods. The vast majority of church expansion projects tend to fall in one of three approaches: design/bid/build, construction management or design/build. Therefore, these are the three that we will discuss in more detail.

Other approaches include traditional, pre-selected contractor, negotiated bid or bridging. The design and construction services within a particular project delivery method can vary. For instance, in some states, it is common to use a designer and then an architect and his engineers, while other areas allow building design by the engineer. Contractor qualifications and the potential areas of responsibility vary from state to state.

The choices become even greater when you consider that there are standard contracts prepared for each major project delivery classification that have been crafted by various organizations, including the American Institute of Architects (AIA), Association of General Contractors (AGC), Design Build Institute of America

(DBIA), among others. The choices become infinite when you consider that in nearly every case these standard contracts must be specifically amended for the situation as well as the number of independently prepared contracts that may be applicable.

Note: The reference to "architect" throughout this chapter is meant to include the services of a designer and/or structural, plumbing, mechanical and electrical engineers.

DESIGN/BID/BUILD

The design/bid/build method is often called the traditional approach because it was the predominant project delivery method throughout most of the 20th century. Consequently, until the last three decades, the vast majority of church projects were completed utilizing this method. It is the approach that many church members are most familiar with.

In the design/bid/build approach, the church contracts with an architectural firm to provide all design services. The church works with that firm from preliminary drawings through the completion of the construction drawings. The construction drawings (sometimes referred to as the contract documents) are then given to general contractors to solicit a bid for the work as outlined by the construction drawings. The church then selects and contracts with the contractor based on a combination of his bid and qualifications.

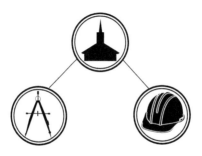

The design/bid/build approach is characterized by the fact that the church is contracting independently with the architect and the contractor. There is no formal contractual relationship between the architect and the contractor. In fact, the architect is normally seen as the owner's agent to oversee the contractor through construction administration. The architect will do periodic reviews of the contractor's work and provide certification on the amount of work completed for the contractor's draw request.

Having the architect serve as the church's agent looking out for its interests can be an advantage. However, the adversarial roles that are often inherent in the traditional approach can lead to added costs through conflicts in the drawings as well as a greater likelihood of litigation. During the design phase, it also does not normally take advantage of input from the contractor and subcontractors on viability and cost issues. This input could result in a facility of equal or greater value for less money and is normally referred to as value engineering.

The design/bid/build approach can be varied to take advantage of the value engineering capabilities of a contractor. You can do this by selecting the contractor before the construction documents are completed. The contractor is selected based on his qualifications and experience in both the type of facility and this approach. This will, theoretically, build value engineering into the process, and it may ease the adversarial roles by giving the contractor and the architect the opportunity to begin working relationships, though they will still be under separate contracts to the church.

Some church projects have been forced into bringing the architect and contractor together after pursuing the traditional design/bid/build approach and finding their project over budget. A contractor can be selected to work with the architect to discuss how the construction drawings can be changed to bring the project into budget. This is the situation that every church will want to avoid because significant changes at this point often render the facility less useful than originally intended. It also means additional costs for the church and a significant loss of time and momentum and, sometimes, credibility with the congregation.

CONSTRUCTION MANAGEMENT

Construction management is similar to design/bid/build in that the church will typically contract directly with the architect and the contractor under separate agreements. In some cases, there may be a fourth party called the construction manager. Often, the contractor will also be the construction manager. The construction manager works on a fee basis over and above what is paid to the architect and contractor.

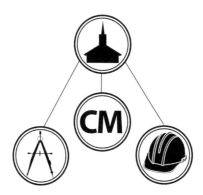

There are probably more variations in approach that fall under the construction management umbrella than any other project delivery method. Some of the terms used may have very different meanings depending on the given situation. It is extremely important that the church pay attention to the details of the contract. The description and the details of the contract should outline the risks and responsibilities of all parties, regardless of the names they may be given.

One approach to construction management is construction manager as adviser. Here the church hires an independent third party for advice during the design and construction of the facilities. The construction manager has no contractual relationship with either the architectural firm or the contractor. In this approach the construction manager accepts no legal responsibility for cost or quality.

Another approach to construction management is construction manager as agent. As agent, the construction manager is playing a more integral role than adviser. The separate contracts with the architect and the contractor will likely flow through him and may be signed by the construction manager as the agent for the church. The church must understand the limits of this approach so it isn't thinking the construction manager as agent is taking more of the risk off the shoulders of the church than is actually happening.

A third approach to construction management is sometimes referred to as construction manager, or CM at risk. Here the construction manager is taking on the role as the builder. He will directly sign the prime contracts for the completion of the work. He is formally brought on before the design is complete to provide input on viability and cost issues. In this way, it is very similar to the pre-selected general contractor approach from design/bid/build depending on the specific role of the construction manager or general contractor.

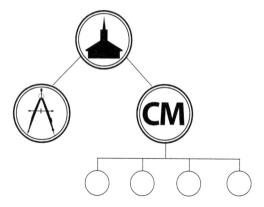

These are just some of the major categories that come under the heading of construction management. If the church is considering construction management, it should thoroughly research not only the experience and expertise of the construction manager, but also the specific roles and responsibilities. That will help the church to understand what will be required of it throughout the project as well as the level of risk it may be accepting.

It is easy for a church to take on much more risk than it realizes in the construction management approach. In the construction management approach, there are many times when the contractor does not give a lump-sum firm price or a guaranteed maximum price. However, I have seen many churches misled into thinking that the "firm estimate" was the number that the construction manager was contractually liable for. Construction management may not eliminate some of the potential negatives from the design/bid/build approach such as adversarial roles.

A construction management approach may mean more work on the part of the church. In some instances, the church will be required to perform the accounting duties of the project including subcontractor and supplier draw requests and approvals and lien releases. The contract may require the church to have input on the actual selection of the subcontractors and suppliers to be involved, which means reviewing bids and qualifications to make the appropriate selection. The church is also drawn more into the day-to-day activities. Some churches relish the opportunity to have this level of involvement, while most would find it cumbersome. It can pull time and energy away from ministry.

The construction management approach often means more risk on the part of the church. In many construction management contracts, the church is the general contractor. It means the church must carry additional insurance than would be necessary in a design/bid/build or the design/build approach. It is also common to find the warranty will be directly with the subcontractors rather than through the general contractor, which may increase risks and costs for the church.

DESIGN/BUILD

The design/build approach began gaining significant popularity in the last couple of decades of the 20th century. While it seemed to be a new approach because it had not been widely utilized, it is actually the way things were done centuries ago for the construction of some of the great cathedrals. In those days, there were people known as master builders who provided the architectural and design services and the direction of the construction. Over the years, specialization in trades gave way to segmentation and the design/bid/build or traditional approach.

Design/build is characterized as single source responsibility for design and construction. This approach seemed to address the added cost, liabilities and litigation of the adversarial roles sometime experienced in the design/bid/build approach. It is generally believed that the majority of private projects are some form of design/build. Many states and municipalities are changing or adjusting laws to open the design and construction of public projects to this approach. It has been projected that, by 2005, more than 50 percent of all construction projects will be some form of design/build.

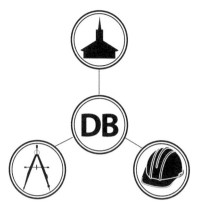

Design/build can take several forms. One is where the design builder is a separate entity. The church would contract with the design/build entity that then may subcontract with the architect and the contractor to provide the design and construction services. For most church projects, this approach is rare. Another approach is referred to as architect led design/build. It is also rare because most architectural firms lack the financial and bonding capacities necessary to take on the construction.

The most common form of design/build is contractor-led design/build. In this approach, the church contracts with the contractor to provide the design and construction. By doing so, the church has one source to look to for the responsibility of the quality of the design, the quality of the construction and the control of the cost and schedule. The contractor will subcontract with an architectural firm that is a separate entity. They form a team to work together from the beginning to design and build the facility that will meet the ministry needs of the church and be within budget.

In some cases the architect and contractor will be part of the same firm. This is sometimes referred to as package design/ build. One obvious advantage of this approach is that the architect and contractor will likely be highly integrated with a great deal of cooperation and coordination. However, one indictment of this approach has been that the contractor tends to dictate design, resulting in bland and unimaginative solutions to building.

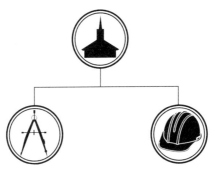

In the design/build approach, the church can usually get more meaningful estimates of the construction costs earlier in the process. Cooperation and coordination of the architect and the contractor allow them to explore the best approaches to achieve the goals of the project. Here teamwork is of paramount importance. The teamwork thrives on the trust and cooperation developed between the church, the contractor and the architect.

SELECTION PROCESS

The first step in the selection process is to decide on the project delivery method. There are various studies out that report one method or another to be more successful more often. The truth is, every project delivery method is capable of success or failure. It is important to find the method that will best fit your church, but it is even more important to find the right people to serve you in this process.

The prior section used three broad categories in an effort to introduce you to the majority of the popular approaches. The tendency can be to look at those three broad categories as the only options when, in fact, there are dozens of variations within each of those broad categories. The precise variation will depend on the specifics of the services to be provided, the quality of those services and the balance of the risk and reward in the contract, among other issues.

You may consider interviewing firms that represent one or more of the project delivery methods in an effort to gain additional understanding into the nuances of the various approaches. A process of meetings and interviews will give you the opportunity to ask specific questions as they relate to your church. You can raise major concerns and priorities and find out how those will be affected by the various approaches.

The interview process, whether for the purposes of determining a project delivery method or for the selection of the specific firms, begins with an investigation. That investigation begins with locating firms with whom there may be a mutual interest in your project. The most common method is through referrals - from fellow pastors, denominational leaders, other industry professionals and others.

Your investigation may turn up a larger number of firms than you wish to interview. Interviewing more than three to five firms can be cumbersome and confusing. A request for qualifications (RFQ) form is a way to get additional information to reduce the possibilities to three to five firms. The RFQ would briefly describe the type and scope of the project you are considering and request information from the firm on its willingness and ability to handle the project. From the responses to the RFQ, you can select those to be invited for interviews with the committee.

In the selection process, there are a few key characteristics that you want to evaluate:

1. Experience – Here you are not just looking for experience in the design and building industry. It is important to understand what specific experience the company has in the size and type of facility you are considering. Someone who is not familiar with working with churches may have difficulty navigating the congregational committee and hierarchical aspects of many churches. Expertise forged through experience can add value to your project.

The company also should have experience in the specific project delivery method you have selected. Misunderstandings can occur between the church and industry professionals when the industry professional is not well versed in the specific project delivery method. Inexperience also makes it difficult to maximize the value of that approach.

2. Familiarity with current trends – The firm you select should be familiar with the current trends in church growth and development. Understanding how that facility may be used in the future will help to maximize its usefulness later as well as meet the ministry needs of today.

3. Flexibility – Every church is composed of people with personalities and backgrounds of all types. It takes a great deal of patience and understanding to move with the ebb and flow of a church. It is good to have a company that is firm in its convictions, but if it too rigid in its perspective and approach, problems can develop.

4. Team player – Whatever delivery method you choose, the sense of team is very important. Be wary of any contractor that trivializes the role of the architect and vice-versa.

5. Character and integrity – It is critical beyond all other considerations that you have confidence in the character of the individual and corporation you select. Experience cannot overcome a lack of integrity. Whatever investigation you do, make sure you can determine the character of those who will be working for you the next couple of years.

The best way to assess these characteristics is to look at the past of the companies you are considering. What have they done that indicates the likelihood of their success? It is important to thoroughly check references to confirm that they have delivered on the claims made in the interview phase. It is a good idea to ask for references from difficult projects, so you know how they reacted in negative situations.

KNOW YOUR CONTRACT

The relationship between a church and its industry professionals is a balance of risk and reward. The contract spells out the risks that are to be taken by each party and its respective obligations and benefits. Our focus with contracts has always been to make them clear and complete rather than concentrating on making them defensible in court. Clear understanding of the contract by both parties lessens the chance of disputes over misunderstandings and increases the likelihood of a successful partnership.

Sometimes people can be discussing what they believe is agreement on an issue when, in fact, they disagree or don't realize they are talking about different issues. I have found that putting these issues in writing will often expose a prior verbal "agreement" as a misunderstanding. The contract can be an opportunity to make sure the agreements reached verbally are, truly agreements.

Another useful purpose for the contract is to bring together a mutual agreement on all the aspects of the project at the same time. During the preparation, planning and design phases, many options will likely be discussed at length. It is easy to become confused about the decisions in every area, even if every member has attended every meeting. The contract gives you a document that brings all of those decisions together in one place. If you are wondering whether the walls in the restroom have ceramic tile, you should be able to go to the contract to answer that question. It doesn't mean it couldn't be changed, it just means that, for the price, risk and reward outlined in the contract, these were the decisions at that time.

There are a number of standard contracts that are published by various groups such as the American Institute of Architects (AIA), Association of General Contractors (AGC), Design Build Institute of America (DBIA), among others. Some provide standards for different types of project delivery methods. All come from different perspectives with different levels of emphasis and, in most cases must be adapted to the specifics of each situation. Many companies that specialize in certain project delivery methods and types of construction have developed their own contracts that may best suit the circumstances.

The contract is normally made up of several parts. The body of the contract will describe the scope of the project and define compensation and how it is to be paid. It will include conditions describing roles and responsibilities. These general conditions may be included in the body of the contract or may be referenced as an attachment.

The body of the contract will normally reference drawings and specifications that describe the project in more detail. To eliminate confusion, identify the drawings by date and author. The drawings should address the scope of the work covered by the contract, including those for site engineering, architecture, structure, plumbing, mechanics and electric. The specifications may be included on the drawings or provided as a separate document. The contract may also mention soil, hazardous material and other reports.

A key element of the contract is the price relative to the work that is to be performed. It is important for the church to understand clearly whether this is a firm price and how it could escalate. I have seen many churches that thought they were getting a firm price only to find out the language of the contract rendered that price nothing more than an estimate or guess. I have found that estimates given by entities that are not taking the financial risk are not very reliable. If it is not a firm price, that general contractor is not taking any financial risk.

Even with a firm price, there are instances that can increase the cost beyond that price. For instance, it is normal for the church, as the owner of the property, to take the risk for hidden conditions on the site. If the soils on the property cannot provide suitable bearing capacity for the building, then the church will pay for removing and replacing that soil.

The resolution of hidden conditions means additional costs. If they are not discovered until after the start of construction, they can be an unwanted surprise. Fortunately, most of these situations can be detected in the early stages of civil engineering with soil tests and environmental studies. However, they do not completely eliminate the risk.

Local code interpretations are another area that could potentially escalate the cost of a project. The plans and specifications on which the contractor based his price may have been done in strict accordance with all applicable codes. But there are areas of the code where local interpretation can vary dramatically from the general understanding of the intent of the code. Fire protection is one of the areas where the fire marshal is given jurisdiction to require conditions beyond the code. This can also happen if the governing authority decides to add a requirement after issuing the permits. These costs will usually fall back on the church.

There are contingencies that come from the contract that you will want to be aware of. Depending on the project delivery method, the church may be responsible for disputes that arise from incomplete or incorrect construction drawings. Or you may have an allowance included in your firm price for furnishings or some other accessory. That allowance may have been set up in good faith but could be more or less than what you need. It is important to understand these contingencies so you know where the financial risks are in the contract and what possibilities there are for price escalations.

The scope of the work should spell out exactly what is expected by both parties for the compensation described in the contract. Look for areas that fall outside the scope that could result in potential additional costs. It is critical to be cognizant of areas that are not covered by the contract. The sample project budget in Chapter 5 identified a few of the areas that could make up the entire project cost.

There are other risks that a church can take without fully comprehending the impact. If the industry professional has inadequate insurance and there is a major challenge on the project, it could have a devastating impact on the congregation. Ask your attorney for advice on this matter.

There are times when a church decides to handle some work itself to reduce costs and involve the congregation. The responsibilities and ramifications for the schedule and quality of this work will need to be spelled out clearly in the contract. This is becoming less frequent because most municipalities require the work to be done by licensed subcontractors, and churches are realizing that what initially appears to be cost savings can actually cost them more.

A church must be sure the work it does fits the overall schedule. When the project is delayed because of the church, the contractor is justified in requesting compensation for the delay. When the quality of the work falls short of what is needed, there can be additional costs to hire a professional to repair and complete the work. Self-performed work also increases the church's liability with possible damage or injury that could be caused by church members. The church also takes on the responsibility for the warranty for any work it does.

I have seen a few cases where this has worked well, providing savings to the church and building cohesion among the members of the church. However, the majority of these cases do not turn out as planned. Of all the churches that I have served over the years, nearly every complaint can be summed up in one sentence. "Everything went well. I just wished we hadn't done our own _____." You can fill in the blank. Most churches say that if they could do it again, they would let the professionals do the work.

The contract should spell out a process for dispute resolution. If the church and the industry professional are unable to resolve a disagreement, the contract will lay out steps, which may include mediation, arbitration and litigation. Mediation usually involves a third party selected by the other two parties to help them close the gap in their disagreement. Normally the decision of the mediator is not binding, but his input into what is fair can bring about a resolution. Arbitration is normally a more formal process that may involve the American Arbitration Association. The decision of the arbiter is normally binding, depending on the contract. Consider identifying a Christian arbiter for an approach that may be more consistent with scripture.

The first step in dispute resolution is to work so that you avoid disputes. Thorough documentation is one of the best ways to avoid disputes. You can never document too much. The more things are spelled out in writing, the less opportunity for misunderstanding. Avoid all verbal agreements. Even if you agree with the contractor that the net of two changes is a zero dollar value, you should still document that change so the current understanding is preserved.

WHO DO YOU WANT TO
BE WITH IN ROUGH WATER?

Here is a final word on the selection of your industry professionals that will have a vital impact on your church. Select for competence and integrity. It boils down to whether they have the experience and expertise to do what will be required and whether they are people of integrity.

Challenges are inevitable in any building program. The only variable is the number and degree of difficulty. If you were climbing a mountain, you would want a guide who had been there before, believed in your cause and could be trusted at every level. It is no different for the industry professionals who will guide you in this project.

Remember, the fees paid to all the industry professionals are a small percentage of the cost of the facility, especially when you include life cycle costs. Yet these industry professionals will have the most dramatic impact on the quality of the facility and how well suited it is to your ministry. Negotiate the best packages you can, but be sure you are doing it with the right people.

Before You Build
Chapter 7- Before You Design

**DEVELOP A
MASTER PLAN**
• Develop a Program
  Statement
• Investigate Site Specific
  Issues
• Do Preliminary Design

DESIGN THE PROJECT
• Finish Design
  Development
• Produce Construction
  Documents
• Procure Permits

SAVING TIME AND MONEY

It is readily apparent that there are a number of steps a church must go through from the time they recognize the need for additional facilities until they begin using them. Some churches will move from beginning to end methodically, taking one step at a time.

In some cases, it is necessary to complete one step before another can proceed. However, several of these steps can be addressed concurrently significantly reducing the overall time and expense in the building process. The shorter the time, the sooner you get into your new facilities and the sooner new ministry can begin. Shortening the overall length of the building process can also result in savings in dollars, time and resources.

A strategic investigation will bring to light the steps that will be related specifically to your building program. With these steps and their associated, estimated time lines before you, you can proactively plan the initiatives to be taken rather than reacting to the immediate need. For instance, consider the church that went through the preparation and planning phases and part of the design phase before finding out that it needed a special zoning exception before it was allowed to build. The church was able to get the exception but only after a number of months of submittals, hearings and resubmissions. Getting the zoning issue resolved earlier would have allowed the church to get into its new facilities several months earlier.

One track to consider in this investigation is funding (see Chapter 8). Preliminary paperwork and legwork can be done to research the appropriate funding source for your project. You can begin to assemble the financial package that will ultimately be necessary for seeking funding.

One of the most critical decisions relating to the funding path is whether to use a company that specializes in capital stewardship campaigns for a fund-raising program. Too often churches wait until the design is complete before they make that decision. Then they find that it takes several weeks to conduct interviews and make the final selection. Once the final selection is made, the schedules of the church and the company have to be blended to find the most appropriate time for the fund-raising campaign. That could push the start of the campaign out as much as three to four months. The campaign itself will take an additional six to 12 weeks. If your funding is contingent on the stewardship campaign, you could be looking at adding three to six months or more to the building program if you don't plan properly.

Another key area for a strategic investigation relates to the site. In many states and urban and coastal areas, approvals related to the site can be the most time-consuming part of the process. That important investigation is often overlooked particularly when a church is adding to a building.

A church must comply with the current zoning ordinances whether it is adding on a classroom wing or a 5,000-seat worship facility. Some churches mistakenly assume they comply because they have been there for decades. However, it is possible (and in some cases likely) that the zoning ordinances have changed since the last expansion, requiring the church to either get a special exception or pursue re-zoning. Some require a special exception regardless of the zoning. It is rare when approvals to further develop a church site are denied, but it can be time-consuming.

Areas where evidence of historical sites such as Indian burial grounds or early settlements will prohibit development. There are also certain endangered species that, when found on the site, render it unable to be developed. A third area would be environmental issues where the removal or treatment of contaminated soils could make development cost-prohibitive. Your lender typically will require an environmental study during phase one. These are relatively rare problems, but they can be devastating if not discovered early.

Connecting utilities can have an impact on the timing and cost of a project and, in rare cases, kill the project. We permitted one church project utilizing a septic system design because the county did not have the sewer capacity to add the church. But the county asked us to hold off installing the septic system because it anticipated having the additional sewer capacity by the time the facility was completed. As it worked out, the church never had to go to the expense of the septic system but simply tied into the sewer. It could have been an entirely different scenario if the church was in an area that did not allow the use of septic systems. What if there was no place to build a septic system because of the proximity to surrounding wells? What if the county was further away from adding to their sewer capacity? It is possible development of this project could have been delayed indefinitely.

Sometimes utilities can add significantly to the cost. A church can be required to extend a sewer main for a significant distance, picking up the cost of the installation of the sewer main as well as the necessary easements from adjacent properties. The majority of projects now require building sprinkler systems, which subsequently require adequate water pressure. There are times when additional costly provisions such as pumps must be made to have a workable fire sprinkler system or fire hydrant. The sooner these costs are known, the more time there is to incorporate them into the budget.

Storm water and wetland issues are having an increasing impact on most building locations. It is important to have wetlands delineated before beginning the master plan so that you know what part of your site you have to work with. Storm water management has become more of an issue because of the increasing amounts of impervious land and the treatment of the resulting runoff. The difficulty here is that there can be more than one jurisdiction having input on how it should be developed. We worked with one church project that dealt with three water management districts. The difficulty came when two of the jurisdictions disagreed on how the storm water was to be handled. Since there was no overriding authority, we had to initiate a negotiation between the two government bodies.

Traffic is another area that could involve multiple jurisdictions. Some locations do traffic studies to determine the impact of development on the community. If a state road borders your property, you will likely be involved with the Department of Transportation (DOT). You may be required to add acceleration or deceleration lanes to DOT specifications that will reduce property and increase costs. If you are considering additional ingress/egress, you will need approvals from whoever has jurisdiction over that road. You may need county or city approvals for traffic lights.

Nearly all sites have restrictions regarding how far the buildings must be set back from roads and adjacent properties. There are also height restrictions, parking requirements and green space ratios to maintain. Adjacent zonings may require buffers in the form of walls or hedges as well as the addition of community sidewalks. Awareness of these restrictions is necessary in the preliminary planning.

Landscaping is another area that is having more and more of an impact on the cost and timing of a project. We have built three churches in an area that requires a three to four month landscape approval process and anticipates the church will spend 10 percent of its project budget in landscaping. There could also be issues related to the protection or replacement of trees.

It is important to know whether there will be any special review boards that will be required to approve your project. Some communities have architectural review boards to be sure the church blends with the type and style they have in mind for the community. There may also be historical designations that require a preservation committee to review and approve the plans.

Renovating facilities will raise some considerations that you want to be aware of. You will likely need an environmental study of the facility, even if you are planning to have it demolished. This study is primarily looking for the presence of asbestos in shingles, insulation, and ceiling and floor tile. If asbestos is found, it may require removal by a duly licensed entity. Renovation can highlight safety and handicap code issues. Sometimes a church is planning on knocking out a couple of walls or putting on a small addition. But, in many jurisdictions, any work in the facility will require the entire facility to be brought up to current codes. It can be costly to bring restrooms into compliance with current handicap codes and to retrofit sprinkler systems, doors and windows to bring the entire facility into compliance with safety codes.

This strategic investigation should also make you aware of fees you will encounter. Those may include impact fees that, in some cases, can be required by both the city and the county. There may be tap fees required by the utility providers. And there will likely be site and building permit fees.

It is important that this strategic investigation be done so that you can expeditiously coordinate the time lines of the various steps and make adjustments in the budget. But it 's important to remember: You are not in this alone. You have hired industry professionals who should be capable to assist you. In fact, in most cases they will take the lead in the investigations. It is important for you to be aware that the investigation needs to take place, that your industry professionals know the work needs to be completed and that you realize the impact findings will have on your project.

SITE DESIGN

Before you begin the design process, you will want to bring together all the information regarding the church facilities. This will include construction drawings (preferably as-built drawings) of facilities. It will also include studies done from the work outlined in Chapter 3. It will also need to include a site survey. As we have seen from above, a number of the issues related to time and cost center on the site. It is important to have an accurate and up-to-date survey to begin planning. That survey should include: boundaries, easements, encroachments, rights of way, topography, utilities, wetlands, flood hazard zones, adjoining property owners, bodies of water, man-made and nature above-ground and underground features, utilities and trees.

The information will assist industry professionals in their strategic investigation and provide the foundation for the development of the master plan for the facilities to be built. It will also provide the foundation for the civil engineer to design the site.

It is important to engage the civil engineer near the beginning of the design process. The civil engineer will likely have valuable input into the strategic investigation. The civil engineer may also be able to provide early insights to the design professionals who will influence the master plan.

Once the master plan has been approved and the general layout of what is planned has been established, the civil engineer can begin designing the site. The important thing to remember is the length of time the approval process takes. Many times the site approval process is the critical path in the time line to get to the dedication of the new facility.

THE BUILDING DESIGN PROCESS

The design process is critical because it determines the cost of the project and the functionality of the facility. This is where the overall costs are determined. The design process can be described in four steps:

1. Programming
2. Preliminary/schematic design
3. Design development
4. Construction documents

The stages represent a flow of the development of the design from early conceptual ideas and directions that gradually develop into specific building plans to be used by contractors to erect a specific facility.

Programming often does not involve the design professional putting drawings on paper. It more often involves a narrative that describes the goals of the process and outlines the direction to get there. The purpose of programming is to take the information that you developed in understanding who you are and where you are headed with your ministry (see Chapter 3). The role of the design professional is to understand that information and design a facility that will be the vehicle to carry that ministry forward. The design must also incorporate specific budget and site constraints.

I believe it is unwise to look to the industry professional to tell you what your ministry should be. That is why it is critical to understand who you are and the direction God is leading you so that you can communicate that to the industry professionals.

The programming function will put numbers to the ministry directions with the answer to the questions of who and how many are to be served and in what capacity. It will help to distinguish between desires and needs. It is not likely that a church will be able to do everything it desires so the process will allow the priorities to come to the surface. Programming will help to highlight true barriers to growth.

A survey of the church leadership, teachers and members assesses the needs from their perspective. This should not be perceived as a wish list where you set up automatic disappointment when they do not get what they wanted. The survey should focus on what they think they need to accomplish their ministry. It should outline what they believe can happen if the shortcomings of the facilities are eliminated. An interview process with key church leaders, teachers and members should always accompany the survey so that the industry professionals can get into the reasons why certain features are needed.

MASTER PLAN, MASTER PLAN, MASTER PLAN

The first step of the preliminary design process is to develop a master plan. Every master plan is unique because it takes into account the specific characteristics of the ministries of that church. A master plan maximizes the ministry impact of the site when it is entirely developed. Since the master plan was based on the ministry direction, it should be reviewed periodically. In that sense, it is a living document to be revised according to the ministry emphasis and approach of the church. Developing the master plan can be a healthy exercise.

The master plan provides the backdrop for the preliminary design of the facilities that are being contemplated for the next phase of expansion. The most pressing needs of the ministry will drive the type of facility, which will then fold into the master plan. I worked with one church that was planning a relatively small two-story educational facility, and the leaders initially felt master planning was a waste of time. However, once the master plan was completed, they saw how moving the location would greatly enhance future expansion.

With a master plan, it is possible to design expansion capabilities into the next phase for relatively little additional costs. Without a master plan, it is difficult to make expansion provisions.

In the preliminary design phase be realistic and remember the budget. Many well-intended projects get sidetracked in preliminary design because more square footage is planned from the beginning than what could be afforded. See the appendix for several rules of thumb that may be helpful in the development of the preliminary design.

The preliminary design phase is a time to be creative in maximizing the use of the facilities to reduce the overall cost of the project and in finding new ways to meet ministry needs. That is why awareness of ministry trends and how to accommodate them are important competencies to look for in your industry professionals.

It is important to stay faithful to the ministry direction and those you believe you are called to serve. Whether the facility is to be simple or ornate, seeker sensitive or traditional, it is important to follow through with the commitment. We worked with one church that committed to drawing 60 percent of its congregation from previously unchurched people. The leaders felt it was important to design a very untraditional facility that would be comfortable for a person who had never been in a church. This was a difficult task, but they stayed true to their commitment.

Near the end of the preliminary design phase, you may want to consider other industry professionals who could have information that would affect the design. Sound and acoustics are an area where outside consultants may be used. If you are considering closed-circuit or broadcast TV or videotaping, you may want input from a professional in that field. Computer networking and security systems are also areas that may require additional input.

It would be important to not share preliminary plans with the congregation until the building committee has approved them. It is not wise to have early designs in circulation in the congregation because if members see something that is part of a plan and then it gets eliminated for reasons they're not aware of, they may feel disappointed.

RELOCATION

Some aspects unique to a building program involve relocation. It will require the services of additional industry professionals, including a real estate agent and an attorney well versed in real estate transactions. Relocation is, perhaps, the most emotionally wrenching decision a congregation will make.

Master planning will also be helpful in the relocation process. The industry professionals can help you decide whether relocation is the best alternative. They can help you evaluate the facilities and contrast a renovation or expansion program with relocation. When a church decides to relocate, the industry professionals can help evaluate sites under consideration by developing master plans on them. This information along with other factors (location of the new property relative to the congregation, cost of the property) can help you make the best possible selection.

Relocation is usually a longer process because it requires getting the congregation on board. Also, relocation projects often rely on the sale of property to make the project work financially. It has been my experience that it takes time to realize what your property is worth, regardless of what is indicated by the appraisal. Some properties in commercial areas with adaptable facilities have sold very quickly. Most, however, have taken well over a year.

Churches that relocate may want to consider planting a new church in their old location rather than selling it. This can be a good move for everyone because many people argue that starting new churches is the best way to make net additions to the kingdom. There is evidence to suggest that even when a church splits for the wrong reason, the net growth from the separate congregations may be more than what would have happened without the split. With that in mind, it is worth considering starting new congregations. I would urge you to consider an appropriate size that would allow you to invest the people and dollars necessary to allow new congregations to survive.

DESIGN DEVELOPMENT

Design development is simply the refinement of the preliminary drawings. The design development begins to look at the practicality and viability of the preliminary designs and what it will take to accommodate applicable codes. The design development step has traditionally been thought of in the design phase. However, as design/build becomes more popular, so does desire to know the cost of the project earlier. Design development can have a dramatic impact on the cost, so it can now be found in the planning phase.

Design development looks at safety issues to make sure there are enough means of egress and proper hallway widths. It looks for code compliance concerning the number of restrooms and fixtures as well as handicap accessibility. Design development also will involve sections, which are cuts through the proposed building to design the components of the structure. This is also vital to verify adequate heights for proposed athletics, baptisteries, projectors, screens and site lines to be sure everyone in the facility can see what is taking place on the platform.

CONSTRUCTION DOCUMENTS

The construction documents are the final drawings used by contractors, subcontractors and suppliers to physically permit and erect the proposed facility. The construction documents go by many names, including working documents, blueprints, building plans or contract documents. They are the culmination of the specific building that is planned.

One note regarding an ethical awareness: I have run across many people who are not aware that all the drawings belong to the industry professional. Industry professionals retain ownership of designs, similar to protection under a copyright law.

SECURE PERMITS

For any building project in the United States, a permit is required. In most places, there are three general categories: site specific, project specific and building specific. Site specific permits are the authorizations you would need to expand or renovate your facilities regardless of the size and type of project you have planned. An example would be zoning approval. You may be in a zoning area that does not permit religious facilities or requires a special exception to expand. Even if your church has been at the same location for a number of years, the zoning laws may have changed.

Project specific permits deal with the approvals needed to develop your site to accommodate the project you have planned. You will need approvals to expand your water, sewer, electric and gas lines. If you're planning to add worship space, you will likely need to expand your parking lot. Depending on your location, you also may need to add water detention, landscaping, site lighting, sidewalks and other site improvements.

The building specific permits relate to the type of facility you are planning. The appropriate building department will review the construction drawings for compliance with all applicable building codes before giving approval to move ahead. This is the permit people are most familiar with.

The industry professionals will be able to assist you in securing all of the necessary permits. In most cases, they will take the lead in getting these approvals. The role of the building committee is to make sure that each individual process is started at the earliest possible date so that this part of the time line can be compressed as much as possible. The building committee will need to make sure that the appropriate industry professionals are following through on their obligations.

Hopefully, a strategic investigation was done and the site and project specific related permits are all well under way. In some cases, these must be completed or at least started before the building department will accept the construction drawings for review for the building permit.

You can usually count on the services of your industry professional to submit for the building permit. They will also need to stay on top of the review process so that it doesn't get delayed. Most building departments will review and redline the drawings with changes they would like to see made. The industry professionals then make those changes and resubmit drawings in an effort to secure the permit.

In some larger jurisdictions, it may be advisable to use the services of a plan expediter. The plan expediter is someone who is familiar with the departments that will review the drawings and can facilitate the coordination and transfer from one department to the other. This person often works with the building officials daily, and that relationship can result in a faster review.

Before You Build
Chapter 8- Before You Finance

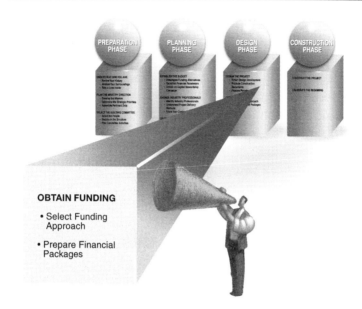

OBTAIN FUNDING

- Select Funding Approach

- Prepare Financial Packages

FUNDING FUNDAMENTALS

A lot of the mystery surrounding borrowing funds for expansion can be dispelled when you understand that most conventional lenders look at two main factors when considering a loan to a ministry: payback capability and debt-to-equity ratio. If these two factors are not adequately satisfied, any other mitigating factor is usually not enough to get the loan.

Payback capability is demonstrating to the lending institution a plausible plan to service the loan. It can be the difference between income and expenses. It is a matter of demonstrating exactly where you expect the money to come from to make the monthly payments to pay off the loan. This is the most important factor because it will be difficult to get a loan from any lending institution if you cannot adequately demonstrate your ability to pay it back.

The debt-to-equity ratio refers to the amount of debt a church has obligated itself to as a percentage of the total value of the church's assets. Most lenders will only use real property, not personal property, for consideration of assets and equity. Each lending institution has its own limits on debt to equity, but it will normally be in the realm of 75 percent. In other words, on the day the new facility is completed, the lender does not want the projected total debt to exceed 75 percent of the projected total value of the church's real property at that time.

The above two factors must be satisfied in virtually every situation, but other mitigating factors also could affect loan approval. For example, the length of time a church has been in existence can have some influence. A church that has been in existence for 25 years is normally afforded more confidence by lending institutions than one that is a couple of years old.

Lending institutions typically like to see sustained, steady growth in attendance. At the very least, they would like to see stability over time. A sudden jump in attendance over a one-year period can sometimes raise a caution flag unless it is thoroughly explained. And it is not hard to see why a lending institution would show extra caution to a church that has been declining in attendance, especially if the giving from the membership is required to retire the loan.

There may also be mitigating factors within the lending institution itself. A lending institution that thinks it already has too many church loans in its portfolio may pass on your loan. You may also be working with a lending institution that is unfamiliar with lending to entities that generate revenues through general giving. If a lending institution in this scenario is your only option, it may be necessary to scale back your project to increase confidence in the payback capability and lower debt-to-equity ratio.

Some mitigating factors within the lending institution might work in your favor. A lending institution with few loans to churches or one that specializes in church loans could give you an advantage. Various governmental programs also could also benefit you. Some programs have required banks to maintain a certain percentage of their portfolio in geographic areas that met certain socioeconomic demographics. If your church happened to be in that area and your bank needed to boost its portfolio, that would increase its interest.

Another mitigating factor could be the positive impact from members or friends of a congregation that have influence with a particular lending institution. One example might be a church member who is a CEO of a manufacturing company that does a large amount of business with a specific bank. Key relationships with bank officials could increase confidence in your integrity and longevity. The combined influence of all the members of the church in their individual savings and checking accounts and IRAs could work to your favor. I have had banks commit to loans if the church is willing to switch its banking to that lending institution and encourage its members to do so.

One other mitigating factor is personal guarantees. A personal guarantee means that an individual or group of individuals is taking responsibility for paying off the mortgage. If the church is unable to make the payments on the loan, then that individual or group will be responsible for the debt service. This is nearly always required when a church has not incorporated. It is more often requested, if not required, of some younger and/or smaller congregations. For obvious reasons, it's a situation that is best avoided.

FUNDING SOURCES

Three predominant lending sources (other than cash) finance the majority of church expansion projects. One would be a conventional mortgage through a bank or similar institution. This would include local banks as well as larger regional and national banks, some of which have departments that specialize in lending to churches. It would also include credit unions and similar institutions as well as Internet sources that fund mortgages.

Another common funding entity is a bond program, which effectively shifts the risk and reward of lending from one institution to a number of individuals and institutions. The lender does this by organizing the sale of bonds that will pay back an investor a specific interest rate over a specified number of years. The money that is initially paid by the investors for the bonds is what makes up the funds the church will then use for its building program. The church must still be able to demonstrate payback capability because it must pay into a pool monthly from which the initial investors, or bondholders, receive their principal and interest.

Over the years, we have come across alternative funding sources that are worth reviewing because they can have tremendous meaning to congregation. One such unconventional source is a member of the church. From time to time, there will be congregations with a member or members who have the financial resources to lend the church money for the building program. This can be a great resource for a church, particularly if it is able to get a more favorable rate or terms. However, the same obvious cautions that apply to personal guarantees also apply here.

For those who are part of a denomination or affiliation, a fairly obvious source of funds would be their own organization. It would be prudent to investigate whether there is a program that would fit your needs. Many denominational sources are for new and mission congregations, but some will lend to any church within the denomination. They typically do this through a revolving fund or denominational savings, investment or pension account.

Foundations can be another source of funding. These tend to be more local or regional than national. You may want to consult a list of foundations in your state to see if there are any that may mirror the characteristics of your situation. If your expansion involves compassionate ministries, there may be funding available through faith-based initiatives. We recently completed an entire new facility for a church in Michigan, where a local philanthropist underwrote the building. The church had to pay only for site development costs and furnishings.

Another potential resource that has become more of a reality in recent years is through government funding for faith-based initiatives. While it may be next to impossible to secure funding through the government for a new sanctuary, it may be possible to secure grants and/or low-interest loans if the expansion is for compassionate ministries, senior housing, adult day care or other outreach efforts. If the ministry need that is driving the building program involves feeding and clothing the poor, welfare to work initiatives or other community development programs, there is a possibility of securing funds through the Department of Agriculture, among other branches of the government.

Some churches have been able to fund a significant part of their facility expansion through wills and trusts. Individual members of the church may desire to leave a portion (or all when there are no heirs) of their estate to the church. These are opportunities I do not see many churches pursuing in recent years. But, they could significantly influence a church's long-range financial plan.

A memorial is another tool that can bless both the church and the family of the donor. A memorial involves attaching a price to a specific item that can then be purchased on behalf of the church, sometimes anonymously and sometimes in memory of a loved one. The following is a list of items that a church used to raise additional funds above the capital stewardship campaign:

1. Sanctuary structure

a. Bridal room
b. Communion rail (movable)
c. 12-foot cross and flame
d. Cross, steeple
e. Cupola
f. Cupola glass
g. Choir railing (removable)
h. Sanctuary doors
i. Spotlight
j. Interior lighting
k. Sanctuary area lights
l. Wall behind altar
m. Sacristy room
n. Stained-glass windows
o. Windows
p. Sound paneling

2. Sanctuary furnishings

a. Bridal room – couch, chairs, full-length mirror, table
b. Carpet
c. Chairs – front of sanctuary, choir loft
d. Chancel area - altar table, baptismal font, Bible stand, candlesticks, flower stands, eternal flame, flower vases, lectern, offering plates, pulpit, two-person pews
e. Hardware for doors
f. Narthex – memorial and special gifts book, desk for books, book and leaflet rack.

g.   Pews
h.   Sound system
i.   Tile
j.   Water fountain

3. Miscellaneous
a.   Fire-alarm system
b.   Landscaping
c.   Parking spaces
d.   Sign
e.   Sprinkler system and well
f.   One square foot of concrete floor

Another alternative that churches have used to secure loans is a mortgage broker. This is an individual whom a church pays to work as its advocate with the lending institutions to secure funding. The church pays the mortgage broker a percentage of the loan but sometimes on a flat rate. In most cases, the services of a mortgage broker are not required. However, if you find it necessary, make sure the agreement is written so the mortgage broker is compensated after the loan is consummated.

CONVENTIONAL MORTGAGES

Conventional mortgages can be secured through local, regional and national banks and credit unions. Some of these institutions have much more experience and, therefore, are comfortable lending to churches. Some specialize exclusively in serving churches.

In most cases, a conventional loan involves a construction loan and a mortgage. A construction loan is money set aside by the bank to be used for the project. The church draws against that balance until the project is completed. Once the project is completed, the outstanding amount is rolled over into a mortgage. A church will typically pay interest only on the amount drawn during construction. Once the mortgage is in place, it will make standard monthly payments, accelerating those whenever possible.

It is possible for a church to secure a line of credit. Typically, this is used for smaller and/or shorter-term projects. With a line of credit, the bank simply establishes a limit for the church to borrow. The church then draws on that amount as needed. The church makes principal and interest payments based on the outstanding balance. It functions much like credit purchases but without the card. The advantages are that it is usually less expensive than a conventional mortgage and can be set up more quickly. It also may not encumber any of the church's real property. A line of credit is often difficult to get because of the higher degree of risk to the bank.

The key elements in evaluating loan products are the miscellaneous costs (appraisals, performance bonds), interest rate and terms of the loan. It initially appears easy to evaluate two interest rates – one is simply higher. However, if you have to pay a significant amount of points for the lower interest rate, then the higher interest rate may be the better overall deal. Points are an amount paid to the bank at the closing of the loan and are based on a percentage of the loan.

You also need to understand whether the interest rate is variable or fixed for the life of the loan. If it is variable, meaning it could change yearly (or more often), you will want to know what the interest rate is tied to. Usually a variable rate is initially lower than a fixed rate but carries more risk. But, it is not always possible to secure a fixed rate.

The term of the loan, or time you have to pay it back, is also important. The longer the term the lower the monthly payments but the greater amount of total interest you pay over the life of the loan. Many churches find it necessary to secure a 20-year term to be able to afford the payments initially. Sometimes a longer-term loan can provide flexibility. You may need only a three-year term because you expect to pay it off in that amount of time but could consider a 10-year term for anything unexpected. Even with a 10-year term, you can still pay it off in three years, paying the same amount of interest as long as there is no prepayment penalty clause.

Another thing to watch out for is the balloon. Many loans are written in such a way that after a certain period of time, usually three to five years, the payment on the note becomes due. This is true even when the term of the loan is shown to be longer. In most cases, banks will renew the loan at that time. But it is important to be aware that they, technically, do not have to renew the loan.

You also want to be cognizant of the amount of property you are tying up with this loan. Generally, you want to tie up as little property as necessary, while the bank will want to be tying up as much property as possible to secure its interest. If your church is in one tract, then it will all likely need to be put up as security for the loan. If your property is in multiple tracts, you may have flexibility on what property is tied to the loan as long as you can satisfy the bank's debt-to-equity ratio.

BOND PROGRAMS

Bonds have been common forms of raising financing for many years. Today, Fortune 500 companies and churches will use bonds to raise capital for projects. Be careful to understand the credentials of the bond companies in consideration since many bond issues for churches can fall below the radar of national regulatory agencies.

One advantage of the bonds is that they tend to be at a fixed rate for a longer period of time than a conventional mortgage.

The initial costs are usually more than a conventional mortgage, but the overall cost for the life of the loan may be less. The amortization on a bond program can run out further than conventional loans, and a graduated payment schedule can be incorporated, both of which serve to reduce the payments in the initial stages. They also may be open-ended, in that additional bonds can be issued as necessary, assuming the church can afford the additional bonds.

Some bond companies have been able to finance church projects that were unable to obtain funding through conventional mortgages. They have a pool of investors who may accept more risk than a local bank. Often a bond company will be more liberal in its interpretation of the church financing and determining what it can afford. Be careful to not fund more than what you are comfortable with. Funding through bond programs tends to be more prevalent when interest rates are higher.

There are essentially three types of bond programs. The first is a best efforts program. Here the bond company essentially uses its best efforts to sell the bonds, but it is under no obligation if some of the bonds go unsold. It will assess your congregation and give you an idea of what it thinks can be sold through your congregation and family, friends and acquaintances. Best efforts bond companies that have been in business for some time will have a pool of investors beyond the congregation that may be willing to buy many, or all, of the bonds. But, if they are unable to sell the bonds, the building program cannot move forward.

Another type of bond program is where the bond sale is 100 percent underwritten. In these programs, the company guarantees that it will sell all of the bonds. These companies typically have a pool of investors that are comfortable with the assessment of the relative risk by the bond companies. Some companies may offer them to the congregation as well as outside investors, while other bond companies strictly sell to outside investors. This program is usually more expensive than the best efforts approach.

A third approach is a hybrid of the previous two methods. The bond company may use a best efforts approach with the congregation to try to sell out the issue. If it is unable to do so within the congregation, it then can offer the bonds to outside investors. The more bonds sold within the church in this scenario, the lower the cost for the church.

LOAN PACKAGE

A key part of securing funding from a lender is the information that you are able to provide. This is the information that will be evaluated by the lender when considering whether to make the loan.

Putting this information together in a loan request package is an opportunity to make a positive impression on the people who will be evaluating the loan. Think about it from the perspective of the lender. Say it receives a request from two churches for loans. One church provides all the information up front in an attractive proposal that is clear, complete and concise. The other provides the information piecemeal, and the lender has to request information. After the request, it takes a while to get the information. The lender would obviously have much more confidence in the information given by the former church rather than the latter. If these were borderline cases with respect to loan to value, debt to equity, or some other mitigating factors, it is easy to see which one would have the better chance of getting the loan.

There is nothing mysterious about putting together a loan package. When you look at it from the lender's perspective, the contents of most packages are pretty straightforward. The information should be complete to the best of your ability, and it should be organized in such a way that it provides a clear understanding of the church and the project.

The best loan packages I have seen or been a part of have had all of the elements bound in a single binder. The binder is then divided into sections by tabs to make it easy to refer to any specific piece of information on request. Copies of the binders can easily be duplicated for use by the interviewing funding sources.

There are many ways to compile and organize the information that will go into the loan package. There may also be some information that is unique to your situation. The loan package should include at least an introduction, information on the background of the church, information on the industry professionals, contracts with those professionals, drawings and specifications of the project and additional cut sheets on key components of the project and the loan proposal.

The introduction should outline the contents of the loan package and acquaint the reader with how the information is organized. It should provide a narrative of the conditions that led up to the need for a building program and the level of support of the congregation. The narrative would then continue with the description of how this expansion will meet those ministry needs. Hopefully, this expansion has been planned in accordance with a master plan that can also be described in the introduction. This would also be a good place for 8x11 reductions of the master plan, floor plans and elevations of the expansion.

The section on the church background should review the church's history, including the date organized and denominational affiliations (if any). It should describe all of the real property owned by the church, including locations, square footage of facilities or the properties and year they were constructed. Another key component will be the church attendance, particularly over the past three years. The lending institution will also be interested in the resumes of the senior pastor and staff. This could also be the location for formal documents including the articles of incorporation and the deed to the property or properties that you intend to encumber by the mortgage.

The next section could be a review of the industry professionals you have hired to serve you on this project. It should include information of the architect, engineers, general contractor and any other consultants or professionals significant to the project. This is an opportunity to highlight their experience and expertise, especially as they relate to your project. You want the lending institution to have confidence in their abilities to deliver a quality project within the parameters of the drawings, specifications and financial commitments.

The next section would be formal documentation of the arrangements you have with those industry professionals. Whatever contracts you have signed with the architect and engineers, general contractor and others would be included here. This gives the lending institution the opportunity to evaluate what commitments the church has made and the commitments that the industry professionals are expected to fulfill.

The next section would be for drawings that are more detailed and specifications for the project. The drawings should be reduced to accommodate the package format, showing more detailed floor plans and elevations as well as sections, reflected ceiling plan and interior elevations. It may also include preliminary specifications. When the actual construction drawings and specifications are completed, at least one full-size set of both will need to be supplied to the lender so it can do an appraisal to assess the debt-to-equity ratio when this project is completed.

The next section will be unique to a project. In fact, depending on the specifics, a number of unique sections may be added. For instance, a church that was planning a significant addition to an already large campus may be considering a chiller system for the entire campus that could be described further in its own section. There may be significant or unique furnishings and/or equipment such as a computer system for Christian education, multiple rear screen video projectors, television/radio capabilities, pipe organ and kitchen equipment. There also may be special ministries that are to be accommodated with this expansion that you want to describe, including their impact on the community.

LOAN PROPOSAL

The final section in this list is the loan proposal itself. This is the heart of the loan package. This information will be specifically evaluated when the lender considers the loan. The first part of the loan proposal would be a resolution authorizing the church to secure the loan. There should be documentation indicating who is specifically authorized to obligate the church for the loan, and it should give some record indicating the passage of the resolution by the appropriate body (i.e., meeting minutes, congregational vote). The appropriate individual or individuals would then sign this section.

The loan proposal package needs to include the financial statements of the church. The financial statements should focus on the past three fiscal years showing, in detail, income and expenses. Normally the church treasurer assembles these statements. There are times, however, when the lending institution requires that they be either compiled or audited by an independent accounting firm. How this information is displayed and what is highlighted depend on the specific situation. If you have been generating a large amount of income over expenses or have been raising significant dollars in a building fund, then that would be information that you would want to stand out. You may want to show loans you have had in the recent past that you have paid off early, showing your ability and ambition to retire debt.

Listing non-recurring expenditures is another common way to show how money would be available for debt service. Non-recurring expenditures are those directed by the church and tend to be rare. Examples might include a new van, audiovisual equipment, a new sound system or instruments. You would want to explain why those are non-recurring and show how that money would be available for debt service.

The financial statement may not show a balance sheet, per say. But it does need to include a list of the assets and the liabilities. This would be an opportunity to establish the valuations of the real property and other real and personal assets the church may have. You also want to disclose all other loans and liabilities to give a full picture of your estimated net worth. The lending institutions will corroborate this information when establishing debt-to-equity projection.

The final part of the loan proposal section is the loan proposal itself. This is showing what you expect the project to cost, how much you want to borrow and how you expect to repay the borrowed dollars.

The first step is to outline the projected cost in detail. It should distinguish between the numbers that are under firm price contracts and those that are estimated. If you have a lump-sum contract for construction, there should be an accompanying description depicting what is and what is not included. For everything that is not included in the lump-sum firm price, a line needs to be added along with the projection of what that will cost. All other current and projected costs should be included, such as attorney fees, closing costs, title fees, capital stewardship and campaign costs. It may be advisable to add a contingency number.

Once you have the total projected funding required, you then need to list the resources available to go toward the project. You will want to show the funds on hand and any anticipated funds to be raised before and during construction. If you had a capital stewardship campaign, you will want to describe the cash and pledges received in that campaign and how they will affect the dollars available for the project.

After you have the cost of the project minus the cash that will be available before the completion of the project, the resulting amount is what will need to be borrowed for this project. To that number add any other indebtedness that needs to be retired as part of this project to give you the total amount of the loan request.

Then it is key to show how you expect to service the loan. If your monthly payments are going to come from the capital stewardship campaign, previous debt service monies, non-recurring expenditures and balances at the end of the year, then that needs to be shown in detail. Lenders tend to discount pledges and commitments to be received.

By assembling a loan package and, specifically, the loan request this way, you are directly addressing the two key issues of payback capability and debt-to-equity ratio. You are also addressing some of the mitigating factors by providing information on the church and what you have done in the past. This is all part of putting your best foot forward in an attempt to secure the funds you need to go ahead with the project.

It is best to present this loan package in person to the individuals who will be deciding your case. Initially, you may need to meet with the individual who will take the loan to the authorizing committee. Personal presentation will allow you dialogue with the loan officer to answer questions and highlight what you want to accomplish.

Before you leave the meeting, request a letter of commitment that will indicate the interest on the part of the lending institution and list the loan products it is recommending and the potential interest rates and closing costs. It will also list any other specific documentation that is needed before approval of a loan is given.

Churches that are considering extremely large loans may want to talk to lending institutions about a partnership that would share the risk. The size of the loan may be such that an individual lending institution does not want to take on the entire project, but it would be willing to share the risk and reward with one or two other lending institutions.

EVALUATE YOUR FUNDING SOURCES

It is important to explore your funding alternatives very early in the process, even as the building committee begins its work. An early evaluation allows you to become fully acquainted with the options available to you. And it will give you additional information in fine-tuning the project budget. It will also make you aware of the time frames involved so that the start of construction is not delayed unnecessarily.

When you get to the point where you are deciding among alternatives, you will want to keep all aspects of your specific situation in mind. For instance, I worked with a church that was deciding between two funding alternatives. Both dealt with 15-year amortization, but one had higher up-front costs but was less costly when you added everything the church would have paid at the end of the 15 years. However, it was in a high-growth area and expected to go into construction well before the end of the 15-year period, which meant the current indebtedness would be retired. Therefore, it made more sense to them to go with the loan product that had lower up-front costs, even though it would pay more if the loan were carried out to its full term.

There will be other issues and considerations unique to each situation. Commit each of those along with the objective information to God in prayer, seeking his wisdom and guidance. And remember: The less debt the better.

Exhibit 8.1

EXAMPLE TAB INDEX FOR LOAN PROPOSAL

Before You Build
Epilogue- Before You Worship

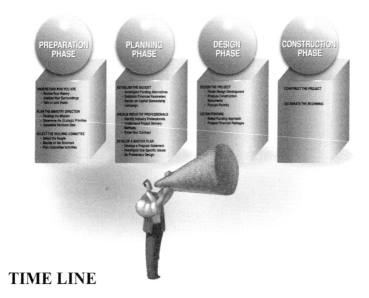

TIME LINE

To this point, I have avoided assigning time frames to the phases because they can vary dramatically from project to project and, consequently, can be misleading. The time it takes to move completely through the phases is dependent on many specific factors unique to an individual situation. The two examples below give us an idea how dramatically one time frame can vary from another.

Church A is designed to be a 30,000-square-foot intricately crafted sanctuary with laminated arches and a wood deck ceiling. The interior includes chair rails, crown moldings and raised panel accents. Before construction can begin, a sewer line must be extended 200 yards away under the road. Bad soil must be excavated, and much of the building pad must be replaced. Because the project involves an addition, a fire wall must be built. Modifications to the old building are needed, but those cannot be completed until the new facility is available.

Now consider Church B. It will be a freestanding 15,000-square-foot, pre-engineered, steel-frame, multipurpose facility. The interior is simple and austere. The permitting authorities determine this is a facility for the use of the current congregation, so no additional parking is required. A few trees and additional walks make up the entire scope of the site work.

It's easy to understand that the relative size of the anticipated facilities will influence the time it takes to construct those facilities. A project twice the size of another will not likely take twice as long to construct. But it could take as much as 25 percent to 50 percent longer. Though not as readily apparent, the type of construction and the intricacy of the design will influence the construction time line. A third factor determining the construction time line is the scope of work that must be done either before construction on the building begins or after it is completed.

The time frames can still vary dramatically even for similarly designed facilities of the same size because of issues in the Design Phase. Consider Church B above in municipality X where all that is required is to submit the building and site plans for permit. The entire permit process may take only six weeks.

Now consider Church B in municipality Y. It finds the zoning requirements have changed, and a three-month special exception is required. Then it finds it is dealing with an architectural review board - an additional 30 days for approval. To get the site permits, the church must receive approvals from two water management districts, a landscape board and the health department. The site permit takes four months and must be completed before it can submit the construction plans for the building permit. If the permit for the building takes six weeks, the entire permit process will have taken Church B in municipality Y eight months more than the same facility in municipality X.

An important concept to keep in mind as you think through the time frames is that you have control over certain aspects bearing on the overall time frame of your project. A church can potentially move through the process more quickly by stacking some activities. For example, say it takes four months to move through the process of preparing, interviewing, applying, selecting and securing the funding. Some churches will wait until the construction drawings are complete to begin the funding process. If that process, for instance, is started three months before the completion of the construction documents, it could shorten the overall time frame by three months.

This could save time and money. By accomplishing multiple activities, the overall time frame could be shortened by six months. For a $2,500,000 project during a time of four percent annual inflation, that could, theoretically, save $50,000. The investigations done in the Planning Phase are critical to the concept of stacking time lines. The better a church is aware of what must be done, the better it is able to plan the most expedient way to get everything accomplished.

There is another situation that, unfortunately, lengthens the time it takes for a church to get its facilities completed. Too often, churches think they're at the end of the Design Phase only to find out their project is over budget. Now it must be redesigned, repriced and, sometimes, repermitted. This is a painful process that can take up to a year or more, depending on how far over budget the project may be. Sometimes the project even dies.

Even when all goes well, it is not unusual for it to take two years from the selection of the building committee until a church is able to step into the new facilities. I find that many churches are surprised by the amount of time it takes to go from "Dream to Dedication." This can result in a church's beginning the process later than it should because it was unaware of the time it would take to get into the new facilities. It can also put a church in a reactive instead of proactive posture, forcing unwise decisions. Underestimating the time frame can take its toll on the enthusiasm and momentum of the congregation and on the finances.

A project that involves relocation can often add a year or more to a given situation. This is particularly true if the relocation effort is contingent on the sale of the current facilities. It can take time for a congregation to understand the true market value of its church facilities – regardless of what the appraisal might say. It also takes longer to bring the congregation through the emotional process of leaving buildings that have significant feelings tied to them.

A FINAL FOCUS

This book is quite obviously an overview of the building process leading to the start of construction. A separate book could be written on nearly every chapter, but I thought it was important to provide the framework for churches to get their arms around the entire process before branching out into more detail.

The framework in this book is meant to give you a comprehensive overview of the process for developing shelter for worship and ministry. It is not meant to box you in or to be restrictive. Rather, it is intended to be a tool to which you can add your knowledge and put to use in the way that will benefit you most.

I have focused on the activities that are part of the Preparation and Planning Phases rather than the Design and Construction Phases. That is because most churches won't design and build their own facilities. They will engage industry professionals for those parts of the process. If they do a good job of selecting industry professionals with the integrity and competence necessary to accomplish their project, then those industry professionals should be able to lead them through design and construction. The right industry professionals will be able to assist in budgeting, financing and other aspects of the building process. But what these industry professionals cannot do is tell you what your ministry direction should be. This must be owned and embraced by the church.

Every church should do three things during a building program that will enable them to leap over the vast majority of the challenges they will face:

1) Be purposeful about your ministry direction (Plan the Ministry Direction).
2) Plan the finances and stay within that plan (Set Up the Budget)
3) Master plan the site and develop the preliminary drawings in accordance with the budget and the master plan (Develop a Master Plan).

I want to take the opportunity to encourage you to consider the option of planting new churches. You may very well see a greater net growth to the kingdom between the two churches than you would have on your own. I also encourage you to remember outreach to the disenfranchised. There are people all around us in great need that we often overlook because they don't go to the restaurants we frequent, or attend the churches we attend, or experience the concerts we go to. But God calls us to keep our eyes open to the poor.

CELEBRATE THE BEGINNING

I began this book with the analogy of a mountain ascent. There are certainly a number of useful parallels that can be drawn. But there is at least one significant difference. Climbing a mountain is usually an event in itself, while a building program is simply a step to put a church in position to do greater ministry.

Too many churches get so focused on the building process that they see completion of the building as an end. It's not. It's just the beginning. Keep your focus on the ministry God has called you to so that when you complete the construction you can celebrate the beginning.

Finally– bathe your project in prayer. There are too many obstacles and hardships in a building process to set out in our will without God. Besides, in our weaknesses, he is made strong (2 Corinthians 12:9-10) and in him we are able to do more than we could ask or imagine (Ephesians 3:20-21).

I wish you all of God's best.

Appendix

Rules Of Thumb-
Space and Dimension
Recommendations

SPACE AND DIMENSION
RECOMMENDATIONS

- Rules of Thumb are intended to provide general guidelines for estimation of property, building space and other needs prerequisite to actual planning. It is not a substitute for actual planning and design.

- A rule of thumb is useful only in making approximations and should not be used dogmatically. Understanding the variables affecting their values is essential in their application to specific situations.

SITE PLANNING
- Facilities for worship, education, fellowship, administration and parking:
- 1 acre per 100-125 in attendance on site at one time.
- Outdoor recreation: 2 to 4 additional acres.

Note: These requirements are based on usable acres. Zoning regulations, storm water retention requirements, utility easements, irregular property shape, steep slopes and low-lying areas may reduce usable acreage.

PARKING
- One space for every 2 to 2.5 people in attendance on site at one time.
- Parking ground coverage:
- 100-110 spaces per acre used for parking only. (Assumes efficient layout with parking on both sides of driving lanes and allowing for landscaping and general access.)

Note: 90° parking on both sides of two-way driving lanes is generally the most efficient layout for parking.

PARKING SPACE DIMENSIONS:
- Standard: 9 feet by 18 feet
- Handicapped: 8 feet by 18 feet, with 5-foot access aisle.
- Van accessible: 8 feet by 18 feet, with 8-foot access aisle (Access aisle can be shared by two parking spaces.)
- Handicap parking requirements vary. Check local requirements.

The following requirements from the Americans with Disabilities Act (ADA) may be used as guidelines.

Total parking	Required minimum in lot of accessible spaces
1 to 25	1
26 to 50	2
51 to 75	3
76 to 100	4
101 to 150	5
151 to 200	6
201 to 300	7
301 to 400	8
401 to 500	9
501 to 1,000	2 percent of total
1,001 and over	20 plus 1 for each 100 over 1,000

Note: One in every eight accessible spaces, but not less than one must be van accessible.

WORSHIP CENTER
General building size
- Up to 300 capacity
  -15-17 feet per person
- Above 300 capacity
  -12-18 feet per person

Note: Rectangular buildings with straight row seating require less space per person than buildings with radial seating. In some instances, 10 square feet per person is adequate in straight row seating for buildings with capacity over 500.

Pulpit platform
- Front to back depth:
  -7 feet minimum; larger buildings require 10 feet or more.
- Height (based on flat floor in seating area):
  - Fewer than 11 rows of congregational seating: 2 feet maximum
  -Up to 18 rows of congregational seating: 3 feet maximum
- Distance from platform to front pew:
  -7 feet minimum; larger buildings require 8 feet or more

Note: With a Lord's Supper table platform of 4 feet, 10 to 12 feet will be required.
Choir area

- Choir capacity:
  - –10-12 percent of congregational capacity
- Choir rows:
  - – 3 feet minimum depth
- Back and front rows:
  - –3 feet, 2 inches minimum depth
- Seating:
  - –Movable chairs at 22-24 inches width per person
  - –Surfaces: Acoustically reflective floor, walls and ceiling surfaces recommended.
- Floor covering: Hardwood, stone or vinyl; Carpet not recommended under piano or in choir area

Congregational seating
Local building codes and the National Life Safety Code adopted by the locality should be consulted for minimum requirements.
- Row spacing:
  - –34 inches minimum, 36 inches or more recommended.
- Row lengths and seating:
  - –Average space per person, 20-22 inches width; 13 or 14 people maximum on each row

Note: Most building codes are based on 18 inches per person.
- Handicap seating:
  - –Requirements vary by locality. The following requirements from the Americans with Disabilities Act (ADA) may be used as guidelines for worship centers with fixed seating:

Capacity of seating in assembly areas	# of required wheelchair locations
4 to 25	
26 to 50	2
51 to 300	4
301 to 500	6
Over 500	6, plus 1 additional space for each total seating capacity increase of 100

- Aisle widths (check local codes):
  - –Center or main aisle, 4 feet minimum; 5 feet or more recommended
  - –Side aisles, 2 feet, 6 inches minimum;
  - –Some codes require 3 feet, 8 inches

Vestibule/lobby
- Serving worship center only:
  - –1.5 to 2.5 square feet per seat in worship center
- Fellowship lobby serving worship center and education space:15 to 25 percent of the worship center area

Balcony
- Capacity: Less than 50 percent of main floor seating
- Riser depth: 3 feet 6 inches for first row, 3 feet 2 inches for the back row and 3 feet for other rows
- Cross aisles: 4 feet minimum
- Other aisles: Same as aisle width on main floor
- Stairwells:
  - Two to outside exits minimum. (One may be sufficient for less than 50 seat capacity). Additional stairs may be desired based on design.
- Balcony locations:
  - –45 feet minimum, platform to balcony;
  - –35 feet minimum, between side balconies
  - Provide clear sight line from rear balcony rows to main floor Lord's Supper table and decision areas
- Steeple height
- Equal to distance between roof ridge and ground level.

- Baptistry
- Inside pool dimensions:
  - 3 feet by 6 feet minimum, plus internal steps; larger sizes are recommended
- Water depth:
  - –Between 3 feet 3 inches and 3 feet 6 inches
- Baptistry floor (above last choir row):
  - –6 inches minimum, 18 inches to 36 inches is desirable

EDUCATION FACILITIES
General building size (education, fellowship, administration, music, and media library, with some multipurpose space)
- First unit building: 30 to 40 square feet per person
- Small churches: 40 to 45 square feet per person
- Large churches with extensive programs: 45 to 55 square feet per person

Preschool

- Space per child:
  –35 square feet recommended
- Room size:
  –200 square feet minimum; no walls less than 12 feet
- Windowsills:
  –18 to 24 inches from floor
- Room capacity:

Ages	Capacity
B, 1	7 to 10
2	9 to 12
3, 4, 5	12 to 16

Children

- Space per child:
  –25 square feet recommended
- Room proportions:
  –2 units wide by 3 units long
- Windowsills:
  –18 to 30 inches from floor
- Room capacity:
  –24 maximum

Youth

- Space per person:
  –Classrooms: 12 square feet recommended
  –Department rooms: 10 square feet recommended
  –Multiuse classrooms/department rooms: 18 to 22 square feet recommended

Adults

- Space per person:
  –Classrooms: 12 square feet recommended
  –Department Rooms: 10 square feet recommended
  –Multiuse classrooms/department rooms: 18 to 22 square feet recommended

Weekday child care

- Space per child:
  –35 square feet, or as required by codes.
  –Play yard: 75 square feet per child minimum, or as required by codes.
  –Rooms usually require grade level location, often with direct access to exits. Check codes.
  Check state and local codes for detailed requirements.

CHURCH RECREATION BUILDING
Overall building size
- Gymnasium:
  –with junior high school basketball court, restrooms, central desk and storage only:
  –Building: 50 feet x 96 feet, 4,800 square feet minimum 64 feet x 110 feet, 7,404 square feet preferred with high school basketball court, restrooms, central desk and storage only
  –Building: 58 feet x 106 feet, 6,148 square feet minimum 72 feet x 120 feet, 8,640 square feet preferred With activities rooms, lounges, multipurpose, rooms, crafts rooms, restrooms, dressing rooms, central desk, exercise rooms, storage, etc.: 10,000 to 20,000 square feet. Note: The recreation building can be reduced in square footage and in height and still accommodate a broad recreational program for all age groups, if space is not provided for basketball and volleyball.

General requirements
- Basketball court: Clear ceiling height, 20 feet minimum, 25 feet desirable Side and end lanes, 3 feet minimum, 10 feet preferred High school court: 50 feet by 84 feet
- Room size: 70 feet by 104 feet preferred, (7, 280 square feet) plus 3 feet for each additional row of spectator seating
- Junior high court:
  42 feet by 74 feet (For most churches, a junior high size court is not recommended)
- Room size: 62 feet by 94 feet preferred, (5, 828 square feet) plus 3 feet for each additional row of spectator seating
- Handball/racquetball court: 20 feet by 40 feet, 20 feet ceiling height
- Game rooms: 24 feet by 30 feet to 40 feet by 60 feet or more
- Group meeting rooms; 15 square feet per person

- Storage: Direct access from the gymnasium, with double wide doors for roll in table/chair carts Separate storage spaces for recreational equipment, crafts supplies, kitchen pantry and janitorial supplies and equipment
- Restrooms for gymnasium area in addition to minimum number in preceding chart. Showers if desired with dressing space and locker.

ADDITIONAL FACILITIES
Administrative
- Pastor's study: 250 to 325 square feet recommended; 140 s quare feet minimum
- Staff offices: 150 to 200 square feet recommended; 120 square feet minimum
- Other office space, based on church needs: Offices for support staff, workroom(s), reception area, storage, restrooms, lounge, kitchenette.

Music
- Rehearsal room:15 to 20 square feet per person. Capacity at least 10 percent more than worship center choir area.
- Robing rooms: 4 to 6 square feet per person
- Music library: 1 to 2 square feet per choir member
- Orchestral rehearsal room: 25 square feet per person
- Handbell rehearsal room: 20 feet by 30 feet desirable (allows for a five octave set of handbells with 12 ringers, 32 feet of tables)
- Individual practice rooms: 10 to 15 people at 10 square feet per person
- Voice and Piano Practice Rooms: 8 feet by 10 feet minimum Media Library
- Size: 2 square feet per person based on capacity of educational building is recommended; minimum of 1 square foot per person

Fellowship hall
- Dining Capacity: 1/3 to 1/2 educational building capacity recommended. Some rural and newer churches may require greater capacity.
- Space required for table seating: 12 square feet per person recommended, 10 square feet per person minimum, 15 square feet for round tables

- Stage requires additional space
- Institutional kitchen: 1/4 to 1/3 size of dining area

Restrooms
Minimum number of fixtures must comply with local codes.
The following chart contains recommended guidelines:

Building capacity	Women WC	L	Men WC	U	L
Up to 50	2	1	1	1	1
51-100	3	1	2	1	1
101-200	4	2	2	2	2
201-400	5	2	3	2	2
401-650	7	3	4	3	3
651-900	10	4	5	5	4
901-1,200	12	5	6	6	5

Preschool rooms should have direct access to a restroom (which can be shared by two preschool rooms)

Where space permits, for the convenience of parents, churches are encouraged to provide a diaper changing table in at least one restroom for each gender.

Handicap access must comply with codes, usually required at least one fixture of each type to be accessible to wheelchairs in each public restroom.

OTHER BUILDING ISSUES
Mechanical equipment rooms
- Space requirements vary with region and equipment type
- Consider equipment and air flow noise in the worship center
- Zone equipment so various program areas can be heated and cooled independently

Custodial closets
- Provide one closet for each approximate 15,000 square feet of building
- No building area should be farther than 200 feet from a closet with a sink

- Provide a minimum of one closet for each major building area and each building level
- Preferred locations: between restrooms, near heavy traffic areas, near elevators

Provisions for handicap people

Requirements vary by state and locale. Many codes are based on standards developed by the American National Standards Institute (ANSI), the State Building Codes, or the Americans with Disabilities Act (ADA).

Considerations include:
- Extra wide parking spaces (see parking)
- Building entry: No Steps: provide ramp if steps are needed
- Clearances: 36 inches min. door width
- 5 feet min. hallway width for two wheelchairs
- 5 feet, 6 inches min. hallway width to allow for two people on crutches: restroom dimensions to allow min. 5 foot turning radius for wheelchair
- Slope of walks: Not more than 1 foot in 20 feet
- Slope of ramps: Not more than 1 inch in 12 inches
- Handrails at ramps; grab bars in toilet stalls
- Wheelchair spaces in the worship center
- Elevators

Exhibit 5-4

**Suggested Questions When Interviewing
Capital Stewardship Organizations**

1. List the companies you will be interviewing.

Name   Address   Representative

a._____

b._____

c._____

2. Company information
  a. How long have you been conducting campaigns?
  b. How many campaigns have you conducted?
  c. Are you a member of the American Association of Fund-Raising Counsel (AAFRC)?

3. Staff information
  a. What is the size of your staff?
  b. How many full-time field consultants do you employ?
  c. Can we select the consultant who will work with us?
  d. How many programs has our consultant led?
  e. What kind of backup support do you offer in the event that our consultant is unable to make a meeting?
  f. Through what means will we have access to our consultant? (i.e., e-mail, voice mail, pager, etc.)

4. The process/program
  a. Do you customize your approach for each church? How?
  b. What alternative methods do you offer, if any, for accomplishing each phase of the campaign?
  c. Does your program/process build upon biblical principles of stewardship? Please illustrate.
  d. What part will our pastor and laity have in the program?
  e. What percentage of our congregation will you seek to involve in the work of the campaign?
  f. How many days will our consultant be on site during the program?

g. Approximately how many training sessions will our consultant lead during the process?
h. Do you offer a follow-up plan? What will it entail?
i. What materials/resources do you provide in regard to preaching and educational ministries?

5. Character assessment
a. How did you become involved in capital stewardship campaigns?
b. What are your primary motivations for staying in this line of work?
c. Describe a project that didn't go well.
d. Did you do anything in response?
e. Can we speak with that church?

6. Financial considerations
a. What is your fee? How is it determined for our church?
b. Can we see a fee chart?
c. How is the fee to be paid?
d. What additional expenses can we expect for this program?
e. Can you assist us with interim financing for this fee?

7. References
a. Will you provide us with references of all the churches you have served?
b. Can we also have a short list of more local references?
c. Can we get a list of references from the programs our consultant has led?

8. Timing
a. Can you give us a tentative time line of your process?
b. When could we begin our capital campaign?

9. Summary
a. Why should we select your organization?

Cogun, Inc.

Cogun specializes exclusively in developing facilities for worship and ministry. Cogun was formed in 1970 by James R. Couchenour specifically to serve churches facing the challenges and excitement of expansion.

Since 1970, Cogun has worked with independent architectural firms to successfully design and build more than 600 ministry related facilities in 29 states across the country. Those facilities have included spaces for worship, administration, Christian education and fellowship as well as housing, classroom and library/resource learning spaces for Christian universities and schools.

The stated mission of Cogun is "to provide the greatest value of services possible in creating shelter for worship and ministry." That mission is achieved by valuing every relationship and, with every project, endeavoring to create the facilities that best meet the ministry needs while staying within the budget plan.

Cogun is committed to caring, to listening, to fully understanding the individual church's needs and desires and to working creatively to solve the expansion challenges churches and ministries face today.

**You can reach the Cogun Team at
800-258-5540 and www.cogun.com.**

W.L. Couchenour

Bill Couchenour joined Cogun in 1982 and was appointed to develop the Florida district office. He served as district manager there until 1995 when he returned to the home office in North Lima, Ohio, to serve as president. He continues to serve as president to "The Greatest Team."

Mr. Couchenour received a bachelor's degree in business administration from Youngstown State University and a master's degree in business administration from the University of Tampa. He served Youth for Christ as chairman of the Bay Area chapter and then as a member of the Southern Region Board of Trustees. He was a founding board member of Heartland Christian School, a kindergarten through high school institution in Columbiana, Ohio. He also served as executive vice president of Association of Nazarene Building Professionals.